## IN THE KITCHEN WITH BOB

# Picnics & Barbecues

# In the Kitchen with Bob

# Picnics &

# Barbecues

## Bob Bowersox

Food photographs by Mark Thomas Studio

QVC PUBLISHING, INC.

QVC Publishing, Inc.
Jill Cohen, Vice President and Publisher
Ellen Bruzelius, General Manager
Sarah Butterworth, Editorial Director
Cassandra Reynolds, Publishing Assistant

Produced in association with Patrick Filley Associates, Inc.
Design by Joel Avirom and Jason Snyder
Photography by Mark Thomas Studio
Prop styling by Nancy Micklin
Food Styling by Ann Disrude

**Q** Publishing and colophon are trademarks of QVC Publishing, Inc.

Published by QVC Publishing, Inc., 50 Main Street, Mt. Kisco, New York 10549

Manufactured in Hong Kong

ISBN: 1-928998-02-X

First Edition

10 9 8 7 6 5 4 3 2 1

# Contents

# Introduction

When pavements sizzle and the humidity soars, a meal eaten outdoors under a canopy of blue sky and lush green trees is my idea of summertime heaven. Maybe it's the fresh air, or the liberation of being outside. Maybe it's my connection with happy childhood memories.

Back then, the Bowersox clan would gather on a warm July afternoon and set up a table in the backyard for a rollicking outdoor feast. Aunt Jeanne's Deviled Eggs and my grandmother's Almond Fried Chicken and German Potato Salad were famous even then. As the moon rose and the coals glowed a sultry red, we kids would toast marshmallows and get sticky fingers eating S'mores. No one ever wanted to go inside on those hot, thick nights. But whatever the inspiration, dining outdoors remains one of life's simple, delicious pleasures, a highlight of summer for me. I think it's one of the charms of the season that you can choose either a picnic or a barbecue as an excuse to eat outdoors. We lucked out in America by getting both as part of our culinary heritage.

Picnics probably originated in France (the French word *picquer* means to pick at food; *nique* means something small or of no value). Given the migrations of kings and culture back and forth across the English Channel, no doubt these informal outdoor meals were transported, too. In England, the earliest picnics noted were hunting feasts in the 14th century.

The Victorians really brought the picnic into its own. Picnics during that era in England became social occasions linked to an excursion, perhaps to a beach, a park, or the countryside. Cold dishes to share were packed along in willow baskets and eaten informally out-of-doors in a relaxed setting, a welcome respite from the strict conventions of Victorian society. Given Americans' fascination with the English, picnics arrived on these shores as an alluring new fashion that quickly adapted itself to our country's mobile lifestyle and love of the great outdoors.

Barbecues, or grilling, as some call this happy marriage of food and fire, are often thought of as an American eating affair, although one with a generous seasoning of regional ethnic influences. The word itself probably originated in Haiti where *barbacoa* means "grill." Pirates and rogues roaming the Caribbean may have brought the cooking technique first to the shores of Louisiana. French settlers there favored a savory cooking method called *de barbe et queue*, which meant "from whiskers to tail," referring to spit-roasting an entire animal over an open fire. Or maybe the cooking technique arrived from Mexican *rancheros* in California and the Southwest.

However it got here, it stuck. Is there a difference between barbecuing and grilling? Yes and no. It really depends on what part of the country you're from, or— if you're like me— what your dad called the backyard cooking apparatus. In my case, he called it a barbecue and that's what I call it, too.

Barbecue and grilling styles are regional affairs, distinct in each part of the country with their own ethnic influences, meat choices and seasonings which give them a unique and distinctive flavor. In Kansas City, say barbecue and you'll probably be served hickory smoked pork or beef (think ribs) seasoned with a rub or marinade and accompanied by a spicy tomato and molasses-based sauce. In the Southwest, as you'd expect, culinary traditions from Mexico, California and Texas converge with fresh produce to produce a milder version. Barbecues there don't have the fiery chili rubs famous in Texas where beef is king and "the-hotter-the-better" is the rule. Moving to Memphis, another bastion of terrific barbecue, the meat is pork ribs and the sauce is a finger-lickin', spicy-sweet, tomato-based blend. Pork also reigns in North Carolina where it's pit cooked and then tender slices are piled high onto a soft bun served with a vinegar-based sauce. In the Northwest, close to the sea's bounty of salmon, grilling fish on cedar planks or over a driftwood fire is a tradition learned from the region's Native Americans.

Given our current fascination with ethnic cuisines, I've noticed another trend. Adventuresome chefs are experimenting with flavors and ingredients from Southeast Asia—another part of the world where fire and food deliciously commingle. It's not surprising. We Americans may win the prize for having the most barbecue variations, but we aren't the only ones who enjoy this kind of cooking. In some form or another, grilling and barbecues are an international eating passion. The cooking method can be found in almost every country around the world, from Japan and Indonesia, to Central America and Eastern Europe, to India and the Mediterranean.

In fact, many of the recipes I've included in the barbecue and grilling section of this book have a dash of international flavor. You'll find Asian Turkey Burgers which put a new spin on what to pair with a toasted bun, and Asian Spareribs that have a gingery tang. Or try zesty Steak with Chimichurri Sauce. I promise they'll all delight your taste buds.

Of course, I have recipes for traditional barbecue dishes, too. Who could resist two classics from the South, Hot 'n Sassy Chicken Legs and Wings and Barbecued Chicken? Both are real crowd pleasers, tested and approved over countless summers by three generations of the Bowersox clan. My recipe for Grilled Swordfish, one of the ocean's most magnificent species, is accented by a refreshing Citrus Salsa and tops my list of memorable summer entrées.

With this selection of recipes, whether you choose to celebrate the magical season of summer with a picnic or a barbecue, I bid you *bon appétit!*

# PICNICS

Cold Asparagus with Garlic Mayonnaise

Minted Melon and Prosciutto Salad

Curried Deviled Eggs with
Apricot Chutney

German Potato Salad

Grilled Tomato and Onion Soup

Brazilian Potato Salad

Cold Raspberry Soup

Spinach and Citrus Salad

Roast Beef and Potato Salad

Tomato and Basil Biscuit Sandwiches

Gazpacho Salad

Shrimp Cocktail Sandwiches

Farmer's Market Salad

Cheddar with Fruit and Toasted
Almond Sandwiches

Mixed Grain and Vinaigrette Salad

California Wraps

Curried Mixed Beans with
Roasted Peppers

Open-Faced Roast Beef and
Caper Sandwiches

Waldorf Salad in Pita Pockets

Bow Tie Tuna Pasta

Bacon and Tomato Penne

Feta and Artichoke Salad
on Arugula

Shrimp Rotini in Dill Pesto

Apricot Chicken

Caesar Tomatoes

Almond Fried Chicken

Confetti Coleslaw

Marinated Green Beans with
Pine Nuts

Pepper-Crusted Pork Loin with
Southwestern Tartar Sauce

Poached Salmon with Salsa

Strawberry Shortcake

Lemon Cookies

Kahlúa-Soaked Berries with
Toasted Pound Cake

Peanut Butter Chocolate Chip
Cookies

Black and White Brownies

Lemon Squares

Lemonade

Orange Gingered Ice Tea

When my roaming mood strikes and calls me and my family into the great outdoors, nothing beats a picnic. We have our picnic rituals and a favorite spot on the lake, so our big wicker basket is always ready to go, packed with all the utensils, just minus the food, of course.

To give you an idea of what I'd recommend as standard picnic items, our basket contains heavy-duty, reusable plastic plates, plastic glasses or mugs, tablecloth or blanket (with a water-proof ground cover to go under it), sturdy plastic utensils (or the real thing if you have a spare set), serving utensils, corkscrew, bottle opener, can opener, small cutting board, paper towels, paper napkins (and more paper napkins, just in case!), small sealable salt and pepper set, and garbage bags for stashing dirty plates and trash. It doesn't hurt to include some bug spray and premoistened towelettes either. But those are our picnic basics. It is possible, of course, to have a thoroughly elegant picnic and take the good china and crystal wine glasses, but I prefer to keep it simple. Now a picnic is not a barbecue. Food for picnics is always cooked in advance, packed to travel in tightly sealed containers, and carried to the site ready to eat. Please note that coolers are designed to keep food cold, not make it cold. Pre-chill everything that goes into them that you want to stay cold and don't pack things too tightly. Air needs to circulate. On the other hand, hot food will stay hot if preheated and wrapped tightly in heavy foil, then in layers of newspaper. Use common sense and protect breakable containers by wrapping them in a towel if you must use them, but plastic is worry-free.

When it comes to picnic fare, the menu can be as simple and classic all-American as peanut butter and jelly sandwiches. Or the dishes can have exciting new twists that play with flavors and seasonings to delight the taste buds. Either way, for your picnic dining pleasure, I've included a selection of perfect starters from savory Curried Deviled Eggs paired with sweet Apricot Chutney, to Minted Melon and Prosciutto Salad, a classic combination that's always refreshing.

My main course suggestions for picnics range from easy sandwiches to elegant dishes. In the sandwich category, there's Waldorf Salad in Pita Pockets where the classic apple-chicken salad mixture serves as a filler in a trendy sandwich. To impress your picnic guests and raise the standard for picnic food, serve hearty Pepper-Crusted Pork Loin with Southwestern Tartar Sauce, or Poached Salmon with Salsa at your next outing. Any of the side dishes like Mixed Grain and Vinaigrette Salad, Spinach and Citrus Salad or Confetti Cole slaw can round out a delightful picnic menu.

A picnic wouldn't be complete without some delectable sweet to enjoy while lying back on the grass and watching the clouds roll by, one of my favorite picnic pastimes. I predict no one will be able to resist a classic Strawberry Shortcake that's best if the berries are local. Of course, I had to include Lemon Squares, a bar cookie so popular in my family that I once had to arm wrestle my brother to win the right to eat the last one on the plate!

# Cold Asparagus with Garlic Mayonnaise

SERVES 4

*PEELING ASPARAGUS IS A STEP most people don't realize will turn a thick, stringy stalk into a tender, more delicate one. It may feel strange at first to eat asparagus with your fingers—most Americans aren't used to it—but it adds to the enjoyment of devouring long stalks of one of summer's favorite vegetables.*

2  pounds asparagus

5  garlic cloves, minced

1  tablespoon salt

1  cup mayonnaise

1  tablespoon extra-virgin olive oil

2  tablespoons fresh lemon juice

1  teaspoon freshly ground pepper

Keeping the asparagus as long as possible, trim off the thick end of the stalks. Using a peeler and working from an inch below the tip to the end, remove the outside layer of skin. Turn until the entire spear is peeled.

Bring a wide sauté pan filled with salted water to a boil. Add the asparagus, cover with a lid and return to a boil. As soon as the water boils again, remove the lid and let simmer for 4 to 5 minutes. Gently lift the asparagus from the pan and run under cold water. Place on a sheet pan layered with paper towels, cover with plastic wrap and refrigerate until ready to use.

Chop the garlic with the salt until it is almost a paste. In a small mixing bowl, combine the mayonnaise, garlic paste, olive oil, lemon juice and pepper. Stir until well combined. Cover and chill. Serve along with the asparagus as a dipping sauce.

# Minted Melon and Prosciutto Salad

SERVES 4

*FIND THE FRESHEST RIPE MELON in season and the best Italian prosciutto sliced as thinly as possible and combine them with newly picked mint and you've got the essence of summer. This salad is refreshing, aromatic and beautiful to look at. The slight saltiness of the prosciutto brings the sweetness of the melon to its height and the mint adds a pungent burst of coolness.*

1  ripe melon (such as cantaloupe, honeydew or Cranshaw)

8  slices prosciutto

Zest of 1 lemon

½  teaspoon freshly ground pepper

Juice of 1 lemon

1  bunch mint

Remove the skin and seeds from the melon. Cut into bite-size cubes and place in a mixing bowl.

Stack the prosciutto and cut into a fine julienne. Carefully separate the pieces and sprinkle them over the melon.

Remove the zest from the lemon and add it to the melon mixture. Add the pepper. Squeeze the juice over it all.

Pick enough mint leaves to fill a ¼ cup measure. Lightly chop them and sprinkle over the melon mixture. Toss, seal in a plastic container and chill until ready to serve.

# Curried Deviled Eggs with Apricot Chutney

MAKES 12 STUFFED HALVES

*MOST OF US HAVE FOND MEMORIES of deviled eggs as a classic picnic food. Here is one with an international twist and a slightly grown-up flavor. The sweet and savory combination awakens the appetite and lends a festive quality to a picnic. The suggestions that follow the recipe are just the beginning of all the terrific variations that are possible for deviled eggs.*

6   hard-boiled eggs

1   tablespoon butter, softened

3   tablespoons mayonnaise

2   teaspoons curry powder

1   teaspoon minced green onion

¼   cup apricot jam

⅛   teaspoon cayenne pepper

1   tablespoon minced fresh cilantro

Cilantro sprigs for garnish

Peel the shells from the eggs and slice the eggs in half. Cut a small sliver of white from the bottom of each egg so that the filled eggs will be steady. Remove the yolks and press them through a fine sieve.

In a small bowl, mix the butter, mayonnaise, curry powder and green onion. Add to the egg yolks and stir to combine. Chill for at least 15 minutes.

While the yolk mixture is chilling, combine the apricot jam, cayenne pepper and minced cilantro to make the chutney. Hold in a small sealed container. Pick off enough whole cilantro leaves to use as a garnish. Wrap them in a damp paper towel and store in a small plastic bag.

Using either a teaspoon or pastry bag fitted with a star tip, spoon or pipe the yolk mixture back into the egg white halves. Place the stuffed eggs on a damp paper towel in a shallow plastic container. Refrigerate until ready to pack for your picnic.

At the picnic, top the eggs with about ½ teaspoon of the chutney and a whole cilantro leaf.

**VARIATIONS:**

Use 1 tablespoon of Dijon-style mustard instead of the curry powder. Garnish with finely chopped onion.

Or, substitute 2 teaspoons of anchovy paste with minced roasted red pepper as a garnish.

# Grilled Tomato and Onion Soup

SERVES 6

*THE FLAVORS OF THE GRILL COME right through in this sweet and tangy, cold soup. It is a surprise flavor that is reminiscent of the French onion soup we all adore, but here is presented in a manageable way for a picnic. This is also a terrific soup for dieters in that it is very filling, low-fat and full of nutrients.*

2 medium onions

1 tablespoon olive oil

6 large ripe tomatoes

1 4-inch piece French bread

2 tablespoons olive oil

10 ounces chicken broth

2 teaspoons salt

1 teaspoon freshly ground pepper

4 tablespoons chopped fresh basil

Peel and cut the onions into ½-inch slices. Brush the slices with the 1 tablespoon of olive oil and place over high heat on a grill. Sear on both sides and then move to the edges of the grill where the heat is lower. Remove the black eye from each tomato and cut them in half. Place them cut side down onto the grill. Once sear marks appear, turn them over and put on a piece of aluminum foil placed on the grill. Put the lid of the grill down and cook for 5 minutes.

Cut the French bread into 1-inch slices and brush with the 2 tablespoons of olive oil. Place on the grill and lightly toast each side.

Remove the onions, tomatoes and bread from the grill. Slip the skins off of the tomatoes and discard. Cut the bread into pieces and place in the bowl of a food processor. Pulse until it becomes crumbs. Remove from the bowl and set aside. Place the onions and tomatoes in the food processor and pulse until smooth. Add the chicken broth. Season with the salt and pepper. Slowly add the breadcrumbs. Add only enough to slightly thicken the soup. You may not need to use all of the breadcrumbs.

Pour the soup into a large container with a tight lid. Place the chopped basil in a small plastic bag and use as a garnish when the soup is served.

# Cold Raspberry Soup

*IN SCANDINAVIAN COUNTRIES, cold berry soup is a summer staple. Raspberries really are the essence of summer no matter where you live. This soup couldn't be easier and is really quick to prepare and pack for a spontaneous summer outing.*

| | |
|---|---|
| 1 | pint water |
| ¼ | cup honey |
| 2 | pints fresh raspberries |
| 2 | teaspoons lemon juice |
| 4 | tablespoons sour cream |

In a small saucepot, bring the water and honey to a boil. Stir and cook until the honey is dissolved in the water.

Place the raspberries and lemon juice in the bowl of a food processor. Pulse until the fruit is liquid. Remove and press through a fine sieve into a medium mixing bowl. Discard the seeds. Using a wire whisk, combine the honey-water and fruit.

Pour the soup into a large container with a tight lid. Place the sour cream in a small, tightly closed container and use as a garnish when the soup is served.

# Roast Beef and Potato Salad

SERVES 4

*HERE IS A SALAD THAT IS A MEAL in itself, making it an efficient one to bring along on a picnic. Many people are shy about beets. On their own, they are often too strongly flavored, but in a combination like this they act as a sweet, tender flavor enhancer.*

1   pound red potatoes, cut into
    ¾-inch cubes

½   cup plain yogurt

2   tablespoons mayonnaise

3   to 4 tablespoons chopped fresh dill

3   tablespoons horseradish
    (chopped, not creamy)

1   tablespoon cider vinegar
    Salt and freshly ground pepper to taste

1   cucumber, peeled, seeded,
    thinly sliced

6   to 8 ounces cooked roast beef (rare
    to medium-rare), very thinly sliced,
    then cut into thin strips

1   15-ounce can sliced beets, drained

In a large pot of lightly salted water, cook the potatoes until just tender, about 10 minutes. Drain them and then rinse them under cold water. Set aside to cool.

Meanwhile, in a large bowl, combine the yogurt, mayonnaise, chopped dill, horseradish, vinegar, salt and pepper. Mix gently, but well. Store in a nonbreakable container and refrigerate.

Place the cucumber slices, beef, beets and potatoes in a second container to transport. Keep both containers cool until serving.

At the picnic add the dressing to the salad and toss well to coat.

# Gazpacho Salad

*GAZPACHO IS TRADITIONALLY A SOUP, which can be difficult to eat away from the table, so here is a compromise. If you have any leftover Italian bread (freezing the bits and pieces left over from a meal can come in handy at times like this), buzz them up in a food processor and use as the breadcrumbs called for in this recipe. Toss in any favorite veggie in season that you want.*

| | |
|---|---|
| 2 | cups soft breadcrumbs |
| 1½ | cups diced tomatoes |
| 1½ | cups peeled seeded diced cucumbers |
| 1½ | cups diced green bell peppers |
| 1 | cup finely diced red onions |
| 1½ | cups blanched fresh sweet peas or frozen, thawed |
| 2 | garlic cloves, minced |
| 1 | teaspoon salt |
| 1 | teaspoon lemon juice |
| 2 | tablespoons chopped fresh basil |
| 1 | teaspoon Dijon-style mustard |
| 1 | tablespoon balsamic vinegar |
| ½ | teaspoon freshly ground pepper |
| ⅓ | cup olive oil |
| 2 | tablespoons chopped fresh basil |

Spread 1 cup of the breadcrumbs on the bottom of a 2-quart, plastic serving bowl. Add a layer of ½ cup tomatoes, then ½ cup cucumbers, ½ cup green peppers, ⅓ cup red onions and ½ cup sweet peas. Cover and store in the refrigerator until ready to transport to the picnic. Cover and store separately the remaining breadcrumbs, tomatoes, cucumbers, green peppers, red onions and peas until ready to transport to the picnic.

In a small mixing bowl, combine the garlic, salt, lemon juice, basil, mustard, balsamic vinegar and pepper. Using a wire whisk, gradually add the oil in a thin stream. Pour into a clear glass jar or plastic container and seal tightly.

At the picnic, spoon 3 tablespoons of dressing over the salad and then repeat the layering, starting with the final 1 cup of breadcrumbs. Spoon on 2 more tablespoons of dressing and top with 1 more layer of vegetables. Pour the remaining dressing over the salad and sprinkle with the fresh basil.

# Farmer's Market Salad

SERVES 8

*HAVE YOU EVER WANTED A USE for all the goodies offered at your local farmer's market? This salad has endless possibilities for your favorite fruits and produce. Toss it with the blue cheese dressing in the recipe or a simple vinaigrette.*

In a small mixing bowl, mash the blue cheese and mayonnaise together with a fork. When they form a paste, gradually add the buttermilk and then the garlic, olive oil, parsley and pepper. Pour into a sealed jar and refrigerate.

Place the lettuce in a plastic bag with damp paper towels and refrigerate. Put the corn, green beans and fruit into another container and refrigerate. Place the walnuts in a plastic bag.

At the picnic, mix all of the salad ingredients together, pour on the dressing and toss well.

⅓ cup crumbled blue cheese

¼ cup mayonnaise

½ cup buttermilk

2 garlic cloves, minced

2 tablespoons extra-virgin olive oil

2 tablespoons chopped fresh parsley

½ teaspoon freshly ground pepper

¼ small head romaine lettuce, cut into bite-size pieces

½ head red leaf lettuce, cut into bite-size pieces

½ head Boston or Bibb lettuce, cut into bite-size pieces

⅓ cup fresh corn kernels or frozen, thawed

½ cup chopped green beans

½ cup diced pears, chopped grapes or melon balls (whichever is in season)

⅓ cup chopped walnuts

# Mixed Grain and Vinaigrette Salad

SERVES 10

*HERE ARE ALL THE "HEALTHY" GRAINS that we all know we should eat, but don't really know how to make appealing! Mixed together and blended with a vinaigrette and some sweet vegetables, this dish is the answer. It can be made several days ahead and re-tossed just before serving. It is also delicious when the rice is still warm.*

½ cup wild rice

1 teaspoon salt

½ cup brown rice

½ cup barley

½ cup white rice

1 small red bell pepper

2 green onions

½ cup frozen corn kernels, thawed

2 teaspoons Dijon-style mustard

¼ cup red wine vinegar

¼ teaspoon thyme

⅛ teaspoon tarragon

¼ teaspoon freshly ground pepper

½ teaspoon salt

¼ cup corn oil

¼ cup olive oil

Bring a large pot of water to a boil. Add the wild rice and cook for 20 minutes. Add the 1 teaspoon of salt, the brown rice and barley. Continue to cook for another 20 minutes. Add the white rice and cook for 20 minutes more. Drain and place in a large mixing bowl.

While the rice is cooking, prepare the vegetables. Cut the pepper into small dice. Chop the green onions and measure out the corn.

In the bowl of a food processor, put the mustard, vinegar, herbs, pepper and the ½ teaspoon of salt. Process to mix. With the motor running, add the oils in a slow drizzle.

When the rice is done, toss with the vegetables and vinaigrette. Cool, place in a plastic container and refrigerate until packing your picnic.

# Curried Mixed Beans with Roasted Peppers

SERVES 6

*THE RICH AND SPICY FLAVORS of this meal will remind you just how delicious healthy food can be. If eggs are a problem for you, it is not necessary to include them here. The nutty, slightly browned chickpeas combined with the lentils create the complete protein that you would lose without the eggs.*

1 tablespoon olive oil

1 tablespoon curry powder

2 garlic cloves, minced

1 16-ounce can lentils, drained, rinsed

1 24-ounce can chickpeas, drained, rinsed

1 red bell pepper

1 yellow bell pepper

Salt and freshly ground pepper to taste

3 hard-boiled eggs

¼ cup chopped fresh cilantro

In a large, heavy skillet over medium heat, place the oil, curry and garlic. Cook for 3 minutes, stirring constantly. Add the lentils and chickpeas. Stir and continue to cook until the chickpeas begin to brown.

Cut the bell peppers in half. Remove the stem and seeds and place on a baking sheet under a broiler. Cook until the skin turns black and blisters. Remove from the heat and when they are cool enough to handle, remove the skin and cut into ½-inch dice.

Add the bell peppers, salt and pepper to the beans. Coarsely chop the eggs and fold into the beans and peppers. Place in a plastic container and sprinkle with the cilantro. Refrigerate and keep cool while transporting to the picnic with cool packs.

# German Potato Salad

*THE KEY TO A REALLY FLAVORFUL POTATO SALAD is to be sure to toss it with the sauce while it is still warm. This way it not only coats but also absorbs the flavors deep into the potatoes themselves. In this recipe, the heat will help to wilt the onion, making the taste a little milder.*

1   pound small red new potatoes

1   tablespoon salt

3   strips bacon

½   red onion

1   teaspoon Dijon-style coarse mustard

1   tablespoon mayonnaise

1   tablespoon red wine vinegar

½   teaspoon salt

½   teaspoon freshly ground pepper

2   tablespoons chopped fresh parsley

Wash and halve the new potatoes. Place them immediately into a large pot of water with the 1 tablespoon of salt. Bring to a boil and reduce the heat to a gentle simmer. Cook until a sample potato slips from a fork when speared, about 7 to 10 minutes.

While the potatoes are cooking, cut the bacon into ½-inch strips. In a small, heavy skillet, cook the bacon until crisp. Remove to a paper towel.

Peel and halve the red onion from root to sprout. Halve again lengthwise. Cut across the grain in ¼-inch strips.

Mix together the mustard, mayonnaise, vinegar, salt and pepper in a small bowl.

When the potatoes are cooked, drain and immediately turn into a large plastic container with the bacon and onions. Toss. While still warm add the mayonnaise mixture. Let cool to room temperature. Cover and refrigerate until packing your picnic. At the picnic, sprinkle with the parsley.

# Brazilian Potato Salad

SERVES 6

*THIS POTATO SALAD WILL SURPRISE most of your guests. Most people don't think to use sweet potatoes in a salad, but they are terrific and widely adored. Finish off with a sprinkle of cooked bacon crumbs or stir in a flavored mustard as your own personal touch.*

| | |
|---|---|
| 2 | pounds sweet potatoes |
| 1 | tablespoon salt |
| ½ | cup mayonnaise |
| 2 | tablespoons olive oil |
| 1 | teaspoon Dijon-style mustard |
| 1 | teaspoon Worcestershire sauce |
| 2 | tablespoons red wine vinegar |
| ½ | teaspoon salt |
| ½ | teaspoon freshly ground pepper |
| ½ | cup canned black beans, drained, rinsed |
| ¼ | cup chopped fresh cilantro |
| ½ | red onion, diced |

Scrub and trim the ends off of the sweet potatoes. Fill a large pot with water and the 1 tablespoon of salt and place the potatoes in it. Cover and bring to a boil. Lower the heat to a gentle boil and cook for 30 minutes or until the potatoes are just tender. Drain and set aside until cool enough to handle.

In a small mixing bowl, whisk together the mayonnaise, olive oil, mustard, Worcestershire sauce, vinegar, salt and pepper.

While the sweet potatoes are still warm but cool enough to handle, remove the peels and cut into 1½-inch chunks. Place in a large mixing bowl, pour the dressing over them and carefully fold until the sweet potatoes are coated. Add the black beans, cilantro and red onion. Fold until mixed well. Remove to a large plastic container. Keep cool until serving.

# Spinach and Citrus Salad

SERVES 4

*BABY SPINACH IS SMOOTH, FLAT and therefore easier to clean. It is tender with a slight sweetness, making this a good salad for non-spinach lovers. If you don't care for canned mandarin oranges, try using clementine sections, diced mango, or ruby grapefruit sections.*

1   pound baby spinach

2   6-ounce cans mandarin oranges

12  cherry tomatoes

    Zest of 1 lemon

    Juice of 1 lemon

2   garlic cloves, minced

¼   teaspoon salt

¼   teaspoon white pepper

2   tablespoons olive oil

2   tablespoons corn oil

¼   cup shavings Parmesan cheese

Rinse and dry the spinach leaves. Remove any thick stems. Store in a plastic bag with a paper towel in it.

Drain the mandarin oranges and put in a plastic container with the cherry tomatoes.

In a small mixing bowl, put the lemon zest, lemon juice, garlic, salt and white pepper. Using a wire whisk, gradually add the oils. Pour into a jar with a secure lid.

Place the Parmesan cheese in a sealed bag or container. Place all the components of the salad in the refrigerator until you pack your picnic.

Assemble the salad, toss with the dressing and garnish with the cheese at your picnic.

# Tomato and Basil Biscuit Sandwiches

MAKES 8 SANDWICHES

*SIMPLICITY ITSELF! THESE LITTLE SANDWICHES are beautiful, tasty and easy to eat at a picnic. The biscuits themselves can be made a few days ahead and frozen in a plastic container. A little sliver of your favorite cheese or some crumbled bacon can also be added to these sandwiches for added flavor.*

1   bunch fresh basil

    Biscuit mix

2   large ripe tomatoes

½   teaspoon salt

½   cup mayonnaise

1   green onion, finely chopped

    Freshly ground pepper to taste

Pick off enough basil leaves to make ¼ cup finely chopped.

Follow the directions on the box of biscuit mix to make enough for 8 to 10 biscuits. Add the chopped basil to the dough. Roll out the dough, cut out 3-inch circles and bake as directed. Allow to cool and then cut each one in half.

Slice the tomatoes into ½-inch-thick rounds. Place them on a plate and sprinkle with the salt.

In a small bowl, mix the mayonnaise, green onion and pepper. Smear each half of the biscuits with ½ tablespoon of the mixture. Place a slice of tomato on the bottom half of each biscuit. If the tomatoes are too wide for the biscuits, cut each circle in half and overlap them when placing on the biscuits. Place a couple of whole basil leaves on top of the tomato and top the sandwich with the top half of the biscuit. Either place the sandwiches snuggly in a plastic container or wrap individually in plastic wrap and refrigerate until it's time to pack your picnic.

# Shrimp Cocktail Sandwiches

*A TRAVELING COCKTAIL PARTY. That's what these nibbles will make you think of. They are refreshing and as elegant as any a sit-down dinner party would offer.*

2 tablespoons drained cocktail sauce

2 tablespoons mayonnaise

1 tablespoon chopped fresh dill

8 slices pumpernickel or other dark dense bread

4 tablespoons butter, softened

1 pound cooked small shrimp

In a small mixing bowl, combine the cocktail sauce, mayonnaise and dill.

Spread each slice of bread with the butter. Place a tablespoon of the cocktail sauce mixture on 4 of the slices. Divide the shrimp amongst those 4 slices and top with the remaining buttered bread. Place in a plastic container or wrap in plastic wrap and refrigerate. Keep the shrimp cool while transporting to your picnic with cool packs or in a cooler.

# Cheddar with Fruit and Toasted Almond Sandwiches

SERVES 8

*THIS IS SUCH A RICH, SWEET SANDWICH it is almost a dessert! It is elegant and beautiful. The variations mentioned at the end of the recipe hint at just how many combinations work with cheese and summer fruits or vegetables.*

1 pint water

1 pint red wine or fruit juice

2 tablespoons sugar

1 tablespoon whole cloves

1 large firm pear

1 pound Cheddar cheese

2 kiwis

½ cup sliced almonds

4 tablespoons butter

8 ½-inch slices French bread

In a small saucepot, bring the water, wine, sugar and cloves to a boil. Simmer for 5 minutes. While the poaching liquid is simmering, peel and halve the pear. Scoop out the seeds and place the halves in the liquid. Simmer for 10 to 12 minutes until the pear is tender but not mushy. Drain on a paper towel. When cool enough to handle, thinly slice crosswise so that it will fit nicely onto the bread. Place the poached pear in a small, sealed container.

Cut the Cheddar into 8 wedges. Cover and store in plastic wrap.

Remove the skin from the kiwis. Cut in half, lengthwise. Lay the fruit flat and slice across into thin half rounds. Place carefully in a plastic container and refrigerate until it's time to pack for your picnic.

In a dry, heavy sauté pan over medium heat, place the almonds and cook until they begin to brown. Immediately remove them from the pan. When they have cooled, place in a small plastic bag.

To assemble the sandwiches at the picnic, spread the butter on the bread, add the cheese, press a few almonds onto the cheese and top with a slice of pear and a few slices of kiwi.

**VARIATION:**
Instead of Cheddar, use Brie and top with mandarin oranges and kiwi slices.

# California Wraps

SERVES 6

*HERE IS A TUNA SANDWICH GONE WEST! This wrap is a salad and sandwich in one. Add whatever seasonings you'd like. Chopped up nuts and fruit in season are a great addition as is a hot sauce or chutney.*

2   6-ounce cans water-packed chunk light tuna

¼   cup chili sauce

⅓   cup mayonnaise

½   teaspoon salt

½   teaspoon freshly ground pepper

6   fajita-size flour tortillas

2   cups shredded romaine lettuce

1   avocado, peeled, thinly sliced

1   tomato, seeded, chopped

Drain the tuna and place in a medium mixing bowl. In a small bowl, combine the chili sauce, mayonnaise, salt and pepper. Pour the sauce over the tuna and gently fold, letting the tuna remain chunky.

Divide the tuna mixture across the center of the tortillas. Top with the lettuce, avocado and tomato. Tightly roll up and cover in plastic wrap. Refrigerate until it's time to transport and then keep the tuna chilled with cool packs until ready to serve.

# Open-Faced Roast Beef and Caper Sandwiches

SERVES 4

*ALTHOUGH THIS RECIPE IS WRITTEN as an open-faced sandwich, you might find it so delicious that you'll want to make it into a regular sandwich to pack for lunch. Adjust the horseradish and capers to whatever strength you prefer. Instead of butter, try mixing the horseradish into some mayonnaise or even sour cream as an alternative.*

¼ cup plus 2 tablespoons drained capers

4 tablespoons butter, softened

2 tablespoons horseradish

4 slices pumpernickel or rye bread

1 pound sliced rare roast beef

Pepper grinder

Finely chop the ¼ cup of capers and place them in a small mixing bowl. Add the softened butter and horseradish and mix well. Store in a plastic container. Refrigerate all the ingredients except the bread until it's time to pack your picnic. Keep the roast beef cool until assembling the sandwiches.

At the picnic, spread the horseradish mixture on the bread and top with the roast beef. Garnish with the remaining capers and a grind of fresh pepper.

# Waldorf Salad in Pita Pockets

SERVES 4

*THIS IS A GOOD WAY TO USE UP leftover chicken, or any other leftover cooked meat you have in the refrigerator. If you have time, try sautéing the apples in a little butter or olive oil before tossing with the salad. This will eliminate their crunch, but it will add more sweetness to the overall flavor of the sandwich.*

1 cup coarsely chopped cooked chicken

½ cup halved seedless red grapes

½ cup halved seedless green grapes

½ cup chopped walnuts

½ cup diced apples

1 green onion, chopped

½ cup mayonnaise

½ teaspoon salt

½ teaspoon freshly ground pepper

4 pita bread rounds

In a medium mixing bowl, combine all of the ingredients except the pita bread. Mix well and store in a plastic container for transport to the picnic.

Just before serving, cut the pita bread into halves and fill with the chicken salad.

# Bow Tie Tuna Pasta

SERVES 6

*BOW TIE PASTA IS A HIT WITH KIDS and has the extra bonus of being an easy pasta to eat when not seated at a table. This is more sophisticated than the usual tuna casserole but still appeals to children as well as adults.*

| | |
|---|---|
| 1 | 7-ounce jar roasted red peppers |
| 3 | garlic cloves |
| 1 | red onion |
| ¼ | cup pine nuts |
| ½ | cup olive oil |
| ½ | teaspoon red pepper flakes |
| 1 | teaspoon marjoram |
| ½ | teaspoon salt |
| 1 | 6-ounce can water-packed tuna, drained |
| 2 | tablespoons fresh lemon juice |
| ¼ | cup drained capers |
| ¼ | cup chopped fresh parsley |
| 1 | pound bow tie pasta |
| | Freshly grated Parmesan cheese |

Drain the red peppers and cut them into ½-inch dice.

Mince the garlic and then peel and cut the red onion into ½-inch dice.

In a medium-size frying pan over medium heat, brown the pine nuts, shaking the pan constantly. Be careful since the nuts will burn quickly once they start to brown. Immediately remove them from the pan once they are brown. Place in a plastic container and refrigerate until ready to pack your picnic.

Add the oil, garlic and onion to the pan and cook for 5 minutes or until the onions are soft. Add the roasted red peppers, red pepper flakes and marjoram and cook for another 3 to 4 minutes. Sprinkle with the salt and stir.

In a large, plastic bowl, break up the tuna into chunks. Add the lemon juice, capers and parsley. Toss well.

Bring a large pot of salted water to a boil and cook the pasta until tender. Drain and add to the tuna mixture. Toss in the red pepper mixture. Sprinkle with the pine nuts. Transfer to a large plastic container.

At the picnic serve with Parmesan cheese on the side.

# Bacon and Tomato Penne

SERVES 6

*THIS IS A VERY SIMPLE PASTA to whip up. It includes some of summer's best—tomatoes and basil, but it doesn't require huge quantities of either, making it easy to prepare. Don't use only fresh tomatoes, as the canned adds a slightly marinated, saucy taste that is needed in the overall balance of flavors.*

4   strips bacon

1   medium onion

2   garlic cloves

1   tablespoon olive oil

1   24-ounce can whole peeled tomatoes

2   large fresh tomatoes

¼   cup chopped fresh basil

1   pound penne

    Freshly grated Parmesan cheese

Cut the bacon crosswise into ½-inch strips. Peel and dice the onion and mince the garlic.

In a large, heavy skillet over medium heat, cook the bacon in the olive oil until it begins to brown. Lower the heat and add the onion and garlic. Sauté until the onion is translucent. Add the canned tomatoes and crush them with the back of a spoon. Dice the fresh tomatoes and add to the rest of the sauce. Bring the sauce to a gentle simmer and then turn off the heat. Stir in the basil.

While making the sauce, place a pot of salted water on to boil. Add the penne and cook until it's tender. Drain and toss with the tomato sauce. When the pasta and sauce have cooled, place in a large plastic container and refrigerate until packing your picnic. Serve with the Parmesan cheese.

# Feta and Artichoke Salad on Arugula

SERVES 4

*THIS IS A FILLING SALAD FULL OF robust flavors. A loaf of crusty French bread and a cold glass of dry white wine makes it a wonderful picnic lunch. Other cheeses, such as blue or chevre can be added to or used instead of the feta. Toasted nuts or croutons also blend well with all of these flavors.*

¼ cup crumbled feta cheese
1 10-ounce can artichoke hearts, drained
12 cherry tomatoes
12 pitted black olives
3 green onions
2 tablespoons chopped fresh parsley
Juice of 1 lemon
¼ cup olive oil
½ teaspoon freshly ground pepper
1 pound arugula

Place the feta in a small plastic container. Coarsely chop the artichoke hearts. Halve the cherry tomatoes. Coarsely chop the olives. Thinly slice the green onions. Add them all to the feta. Sprinkle with the parsley.

Whisk together the lemon juice, olive oil and pepper. Pour it over the feta mixture and toss well. Cover and refrigerate until ready to pack your picnic.

Rinse and dry the arugula and place in a plastic bag with a paper towel. Refrigerate.

At the picnic, place the arugula on each plate and top with the feta mixture.

# Shrimp Rotini in Dill Pesto

SERVES 6

*MOST OF US KNOW PESTO as a basil sauce. Fresh dill, paired with walnuts, garlic and cream, is as pungent as any basil sauce, yet also blends well with the shrimp. If you have time, lightly toasting the walnuts will give added flavor to the pesto.*

- 1 **pound rotini**
- 2 **cups chopped fresh dill**
- ½ **cup olive oil**
- 2 **garlic cloves**
- 2 **tablespoons chopped walnuts**
- ¼ **cup grated Parmesan cheese**
- ¼ **cup heavy cream**
- 1 **pound cooked small shrimp**

Cook the pasta until tender, about 13 to 15 minutes, in a large pot of boiling, salted water. Drain and rinse in cold water.

While the pasta is cooking, place the remaining ingredients, except for the shrimp, in a food processor or blender and pulse until the mixture is smooth.

Place the pasta, shrimp and pesto in a plastic bowl, toss well and refrigerate. To transport, cover with plastic wrap. Keep cool with cool packs until served.

# Apricot Chicken

SERVES 4

*THIS IS SUCH A BREEZE TO PREPARE you might want to make it an at-home dinner regular. Try this with a rice salad or the Caesar Tomatoes (opposite). The tang of the Caesar dressing contrasts nicely with the sweet apricots.*

2 boneless skinless chicken breasts, halved

½ cup diced dried apricots

Toothpicks

Vegetable spray

½ cup apricot jam

1 tablespoon warm water

1 teaspoon sage

Preheat the oven to 350°F. Cut a slit in the side of each half of the chicken breasts. Pivot the knife so that a pocket is formed inside the breast. Stuff each pocket with a tablespoon of the apricots. Pin each opening shut with a toothpick. Coat a 9 x 13-inch baking pan with vegetable spray and place the stuffed breasts in it.

In a small mixing bowl, stir together the apricot jam and warm water. Add the sage and mix until combined. Brush the breasts with some of the jam mixture.

Place the chicken, uncovered, in the oven and bake for 30 minutes. Baste with the jam mixture several times while it bakes. Remove from the oven and let cool in the pan. When cool, place in a plastic container and refrigerate. Keep chilled with cool packs while transporting to the picnic.

# Caesar Tomatoes

SERVES 6

*THIS IS AN "ON-THE-GO" CAESAR SALAD. A lettuce salad is often too cumbersome to handle away from the table, so this is a solution to those Caesar salad cravings. Pour some of the sauce over cold chicken to create a whole meal.*

4  ripe tomatoes

½  teaspoon salt

3  tablespoons mayonnaise

3  garlic cloves

2  teaspoons Dijon-style mustard

2  tablespoons balsamic vinegar

2  tablespoons fresh lemon juice

2  teaspoons Worcestershire sauce

  Dash hot pepper sauce
  (such as Tabasco)

2  teaspoons anchovy paste

¼  teaspoon freshly ground pepper

5  tablespoons olive oil

Cut the tomatoes into wedges and sprinkle with the salt.

In the bowl of a food processor, place the remaining ingredients except for the oil. Process to mix. With the motor running, slowly add the oil.

Place the tomatoes in a plastic container and the dressing in another. Refrigerate until packing your picnic. When serving, place the tomatoes on a plate and drizzle with the dressing.

45

# Almond Fried Chicken

SERVES 4

*Back around the time I was 9 or 10, I remember Mom and Dad entertaining almost every weekend during the summer. Dad would be in charge of the grill, charring the burgers and dogs, but most of us would be waiting in the kitchen for Mom's fried chicken. Being a daughter of the South, she was a master at it. Her trick was to never fry the chicken in too much oil, you get greasy chicken that way. This recipe is an updated version of what Mom used to make, with the rich and sinful addition of almonds in the breading. And if you think it's great the night you make it, wait till you try it cold the next day!*

⅓ cup flour

¼ teaspoon salt

3 tablespoons heavy cream

2 eggs, beaten

1 cup ground almonds

1 cup fresh breadcrumbs

1 tablespoon cayenne pepper

1 whole frying chicken, cut into eighths

½ cup corn oil

Preheat the oven to 350°F. Set up an assembly line to prepare the chicken for frying. Place, in order, a plate with the flour and salt, a wide bowl of the cream and eggs, and a plate of the almonds, breadcrumbs and cayenne pepper.

Coat each piece of chicken, one at a time, in the flour, egg and breadcrumb mixtures. Set aside.

In a wide, heavy skillet, heat the oil over high heat. When it is hot, add the chicken, 2 pieces at a time. Turn as each side browns. Remove to paper towels to drain off the excess oil.

When all of the chicken has been fried, place in a baking pan and cook in the oven for 20 minutes. Remove and allow to cool completely before storing in a plastic container and refrigerating. Keep chilled during transport to your picnic.

# Confetti Coleslaw

SERVES 4

*THIS IS A COLORFUL, SWEET AND SAVORY version of a picnic must. The grapes may seem a bit fussy to prepare, but they give a real boost to the flavor and color of the coleslaw. If fresh herbs like dill or basil are readily available, they too can be sprinkled into the mix for more summer flavor.*

½ pound red cabbage

½ pound green cabbage

½ red onion

½ pound red seedless grapes

½ pound green seedless grapes

1 tablespoon apple cider vinegar

1 tablespoon brown sugar

1 cup mayonnaise

Salt and freshly ground pepper to taste

Cut both the red and green cabbage into 1-inch cubes. Place in a large mixing bowl. Peel and slice the red onion in half, lengthwise, and then across the grain into thin slices. Add to the cabbage. Slice the grapes in half, or into smaller pieces if desired, and add to the mixing bowl.

Stir together the vinegar, sugar, mayonnaise, salt and pepper. Pour over the cabbage mixture and toss well.

Place the coleslaw in a plastic container and chill. Keep chilled with cool packs while transporting to the picnic. Toss again just before serving.

# Marinated Green Beans with Pine Nuts

SERVES 6

*SLIGHTLY CRUNCHY GREEN BEANS, combined with the tang of cider vinegar and sweet, toasted pine nuts, is enough to make you forget that you're eating a healthy green vegetable! These are hardly boring green beans. They can be served cold at a picnic or warm with any dinner entrée.*

| | |
|---|---|
| 2 | pounds fresh green beans |
| 1 | tablespoon apple cider vinegar |
| ½ | teaspoon tarragon |
| 1 | garlic clove, minced |
| 1 | teaspoon oregano |
| | Salt and freshly ground pepper to taste |
| ⅓ | cup corn oil |
| ¼ | cup pine nuts |

Trim the ends off the beans. Cook them in salted, boiling water for 3 to 5 minutes or until they are crisp-tender. Place them in a large bowl.

In a small bowl, combine the vinegar, tarragon, garlic, oregano, salt and pepper. Using a wire whisk, add the oil in a slow stream. Pour it over the beans, toss and store in a sealed, plastic container.

In a dry, heavy sauté pan over medium heat, place the pine nuts and cook until they just begin to brown. Remove them from the heat immediately, and when they are cooled, store in a plastic bag.

At the picnic, toss the beans again and sprinkle with the pine nuts.

49

# Pepper-Crusted Pork Loin with Southwestern Tartar Sauce

SERVES 6

*NOT ONLY IS THIS A FESTIVE ROAST to serve guests, but the leftovers make amazing sandwiches. Or, sauté the leftovers with onions, add some sour cream and serve over egg noodles for a mock Stroganoff. Be sure to save any extra juices from the roasting pan that are not added to the tartar sauce for these uses.*

1 teaspoon ground cumin

1 teaspoon ground cinnamon

1 teaspoon cayenne pepper

1 tablespoon freshly ground pepper

4 garlic cloves, slivered

1 3-pound center cut pork loin

1 cup mayonnaise

2 tablespoons chopped black olives

1 jalapeño pepper, minced

2 tablespoons chopped roasted red pepper

1 teaspoon hot pepper sauce (such as Tabasco)

1 teaspoon cayenne pepper

1 teaspoon thyme

Juice of 1 lime

Salt and freshly ground black pepper to taste

Preheat the oven to 450°F. In a small mixing bowl, combine the cumin, cinnamon, cayenne, pepper and garlic. Rub the mixture all over the pork. Place the pork on a rack in a baking pan. Cook for 15 minutes and then lower the heat to 300°F. Cook for another hour or until an internal thermometer reads 150F° to 155°F. Remove from the oven and allow to rest for 20 minutes before slicing. Save the juices to add to the tartar sauce. When cool, place the sliced pork in a plastic container and refrigerate. Keep chilled with cool packs while transporting to your picnic.

In a small mixing bowl, combine the mayonnaise, black olives, jalapeño, roasted red pepper, hot pepper sauce, cayenne, thyme, lime juice, salt, pepper and pan juices. Be sure to add only enough drippings to flavor the sauce without making it runny. Store in a plastic container and refrigerate. Keep chilled while transporting to the picnic.

Serve the pork slices with a dollop of the chilled sauce across them or on the side.

# Poached Salmon with Salsa

SERVES 4

*NOT ONLY IS THIS A BREEZE TO MAKE, but it can be prepared a day ahead. It is a dieter's delight, but will satisfy anyone's need for intense flavors and a colorful presentation. The salsa is a more-the-merrier mixture, so be sure to add any summer beauties from your garden like peppers or sweet peas.*

| | |
|---|---|
| 2½ | pounds salmon fillet |
| 3 | plum tomatoes |
| 2 | garlic cloves |
| ¼ | cup fresh corn kernels or frozen, thawed |
| 2 | tablespoons chopped red onion |
| ½ | avocado, peeled, diced |
| 2 | tablespoons chopped fresh cilantro |
| 1 | tablespoon olive oil |
| 1 | tablespoon fresh lime juice |
| | Salt and freshly ground pepper to taste |

Remove the skin from the salmon. In a skillet large enough to hold the salmon in a single layer, bring 2 inches of water to a simmer. Add the salmon and cover. Poach until the salmon is opaque all the way through. Remove and allow to cool. Wrap tightly in plastic wrap and refrigerate. Keep chilled with cool packs until serving at the picnic.

Cut the tomatoes into ¼-inch dice and place in a small mixing bowl. Mince the garlic and add to the tomatoes, along with the corn, red onion, avocado, cilantro, olive oil, lime juice, salt and pepper. Mix and store in a small plastic container and refrigerate.

At the picnic, cut the salmon into 4 pieces and top with the salsa.

**VARIATION:**
To make this into a sandwich, wrap the salmon and salsa in a soft flour tortilla or stuff into a pita pocket.

# Strawberry Shortcake

SERVES 8

*THE PURE FLAVOR OF A SUMMER FRUIT such as strawberries, paired with simple, fresh cream, is an unbeatable combination. Little needs to be added to this dessert, yet adults may enjoy a splash of amaretto on the strawberries before they are placed on the biscuits and cream. The biscuits can be made a few days ahead and frozen, before being packed for their outing.*

**Biscuit mix for 8 to 10 3-inch biscuits**

1 quart fresh strawberries

1½ pints heavy cream

1 teaspoon vanilla extract

1 teaspoon confectioner's sugar

1 tablespoon sour cream

Prepare the biscuits as directed on the box. Rinse and cut up the strawberries. Place in a plastic container and refrigerate.

Place the heavy cream, vanilla extract and confectioner's sugar into a cold, metal mixing bowl. With a whisk or an electric mixer, whip the cream mixture until thick, but not too stiff. Add the sour cream and beat just to incorporate. Place the whipped cream in a plastic container and refrigerate until packing your picnic.

When packing your picnic, be sure to include a whisk and a cooler for the cream. Just before serving, re-whip the cream until stiff. Place a dollop of whipped cream on each biscuit. Scoop out a hollow in the center of the cream and spoon in some strawberries.

# Lemon Cookies

*HAVE YOU EVER WANTED to put on an authentic tea party? If you did, these lemon cookies would be perfect. They are delicate, melt in your mouth and best yet, are a snap to make.*

| | |
|---|---|
| 1⅓ | cups flour |
| 1 | teaspoon baking powder |
| | Dash salt |
| ½ | cup unsalted butter |
| 1 | cup sugar |
| 1 | egg |
| 1 | teaspoon lemon zest |
| 5 | teaspoons fresh lemon juice |
| ½ | cup quick-cooking oats |
| | Small bowl sugar |

Into a small bowl, sift together the dry ingredients. Using an electric mixer, in a medium bowl, cream the butter and sugar. Add the egg and beat well. Add the lemon zest and juice. With a rubber spatula, fold in the dry ingredients and the oats. Chill the dough for 1 hour.

Preheat the oven to 375°F. Shape tablespoon-size balls of the dough and roll them in the bowl of sugar. Flatten them on a lightly greased baking sheet and cook for 8 to 10 minutes or until they brown at the edges. Remove to a cooling rack. Store in a tightly sealed plastic container.

# Kahlúa-Soaked Berries with Toasted Pound Cake

SERVES 6

*ANY COMBINATION OF FRESH, SUMMER BERRIES will work with this dessert. The Kahlúa gives a rich flavor reminiscent of the most sinful desserts, without the excessive fat or calories. Low-fat pound cake, or even angel food cake, can be used to keep it acceptable to even the most diet conscious.*

1  pint blueberries

1  pint raspberries, rinsed

1  cup Kahlúa

1  pound cake, thawed if frozen

Sour cream or whipped cream (optional)

Wash the blueberries and pick out any stems or unripe berries. In a medium-size plastic container, place all of the berries and the Kahlúa. Let them soak for at least an hour before serving. Drain and place in a sealed plastic container. Refrigerate until packing your picnic.

Slice the pound cake into 6 or more 1-inch slices and brush the slices with some of the Kahlúa. Toast under a broiler or in a toaster oven until golden brown. When they have cooled, place in a plastic container or wrap individually in plastic wrap.

Serve the berries over the pound cake. A dollop of sour cream or whipped cream is a great accompaniment if your picnic includes a cooler.

# Peanut Butter Chocolate Chip Cookies

MAKES 3 DOZEN COOKIES

*CHOCOLATE CHIPS GIVE A TWIST to this old favorite. Eat one right out of the oven for a melt-in-your-mouth experience, but be sure to allow them to cool completely before they are wrapped up as the chocolate will be runny until then.*

½  cup unsalted butter

½  cup smooth peanut butter

½  teaspoon vanilla extract

1  cup brown sugar

1  egg

1¼  cups flour

½  teaspoon baking powder

½  teaspoon baking soda

½  teaspoon salt

½  cup semisweet chocolate chips

Using an electric mixer, cream the butter, peanut butter, vanilla extract and brown sugar until light and fluffy. Add the egg and mix well.

In another bowl, combine all of the dry ingredients.

Using a rubber spatula, combine all of the wet and dry ingredients and the chocolate chips. Cover the dough with plastic wrap and chill for 1 hour.

Preheat the oven to 375°F. Place tablespoon-size dollops of dough on a lightly greased cookie sheet. Using a fork, mark with a crisscross pattern and bake for about 10 to 12 minutes. Place on a rack and when cool, place in a plastic container to transport to picnic.

# Black and White Brownies

MAKES 12 LARGE BROWNIES

*AND NOW FOR A SINFUL TREAT. Cream cheese cuts the denseness of the chocolate, making them even easier to inhale! Kids enjoy making these and creating the swirl effect.*

| | |
|---|---|
| 4 | ounces semisweet chocolate |
| 5 | tablespoons unsalted butter |
| 4 | ounces cream cheese |
| 1 | cup sugar |
| 3 | eggs |
| ⅔ | cup flour |
| 1 | teaspoon vanilla extract |
| ½ | teaspoon baking powder |
| ½ | teaspoon salt |

Preheat the oven to 350°F. Lightly grease a 9 x 12-inch baking pan.

In a small, heavy saucepot over low heat, melt the chocolate and 3 tablespoons of the butter. Stir just to combine and allow to cool to room temperature.

Using an electric mixer, cream the remaining butter with the cream cheese. Slowly add half the sugar and beat until fluffy. Add 1 egg, 1 tablespoon of flour and the vanilla. Set aside.

In another bowl, beat the other 2 eggs. Gradually add the remaining sugar and beat until the mixture is thick and smooth. Add the baking powder, salt and the remaining flour. Add the melted chocolate and mix well.

Pour half of the chocolate batter into the prepared pan. Top with the cream cheese mixture and then top with the rest of the chocolate batter. Swirl a knife through the 3 layers to create a marbleized effect.

Bake for 25 to 30 minutes. Place the pan on a rack to cool. When cool, cut into 12 squares and gently lift from the pan. Wrap individually in waxed paper or plastic wrap to carry with your picnic.

These may be frozen for up to a week in advance. Allow them to thaw before eating.

# Lemon Squares

MAKES 12 SQUARES

*SOMETIMES JUST A SMALL SWEET is needed at the end of a meal. These squares are slightly more substantial than cookies, but they do not overwhelm as a richer dessert would. Try just one while it's still warm and slightly gooey!*

1 cup flour

¼ cup confectioner's sugar

½ cup unsalted butter, melted

2 eggs

1 cup sugar

2 tablespoons fresh lemon juice

¼ teaspoon baking powder

2 tablespoons flour

Preheat the oven to 350°F. Line the bottom of a 9 x 9-inch baking pan with parchment or waxed paper. In a small mixing bowl, combine the first 3 ingredients. Spoon the mixture into the prepared pan and bake for 25 minutes.

While the bottom is cooking, mix together the eggs, sugar, lemon juice, baking powder and the 2 tablespoons of flour. Pour over the baked shell and continue to cook for another 25 minutes. Remove from the oven and let cool on a rack.

When the pan is cool enough to handle, gently lift out the lemon square and cut into 12 smaller squares. Place in a plastic container or wrap individually in plastic wrap.

# Lemonade

*WHAT IS SO GREAT ABOUT THIS LEMONADE is that you can control the amount of sweetness. You don't have to settle for the cloying flavor of too much sugar and instead can create a drink that is truly refreshing. Garnish it with a sprig of mint or a wedge of lime for color and an added tang.*

**SUGAR SYRUP**

½ cup sugar

½ cup water

**LEMONADE**

⅓ cup fresh lemon juice

⅓ cup sugar syrup

3 cups water

Ice cubes to fill 1-quart pitcher

Lemon wedges for garnish

*F*OR SUGAR SYRUP: In a small, heavy saucepot over medium heat, boil the sugar and water. Stir until the sugar is dissolved. Remove from the heat and allow to cool.

**FOR LEMONADE:** Combine the lemon juice, sugar syrup and water. Pour into a sealed container and refrigerate.

At the picnic, pour the lemonade into a pitcher filled with ice. Pour into individual glasses and serve with a lemon wedge for those who like it extra tart.

# Orange Gingered Ice Tea

MAKES 1 QUART

*THE FLAVOR OF YOUR OWN ICE TEA is a world away from the instant powder we all know so well. It really isn't hard to make and once you've done it you'll probably keep a pitcher for yourself in the refrigerator throughout the summer. There are countless variations to try—simmer almost any fresh fruit or herb, allow it to steep, strain and that's all there is to it!*

16 ounces boiling water

1 2-inch piece fresh gingerroot

1 navel orange for garnish

2 to 3 teabags

Ice cubes to fill 1-quart pitcher

Mint sprigs for garnish

While the water is coming to a boil, peel the skin from the gingerroot and cut into thick slices. Wash the orange, cut it in half from stem to navel and then across into half-slices.

When the water is boiling, add the teabags and ginger. Cover and turn off the heat. Allow it to steep for 5 minutes. Remove the teabags and ginger. Let the tea come to room temperature before pouring into a tightly sealed container and chilling.

At the picnic, pour the tea into a pitcher filled with ice and garnish with the orange slices and mint sprigs. Pour into individual glasses and serve.

# BARBECUES

Potato Skins with Bacon, Cheddar and Sour Cream

Summer's Best Pizza

Zucchini Boats with Blue Cheese, Walnuts and Pears

Grilled Sweet and Spicy Salmon

Grilled Chicken Wrapped with Green Onions

Steak with Chimichurri Sauce

Bruschetta

Moroccan Leg of Lamb

Hot 'n Sassy Chicken Legs and Wings

Cilantro Shrimp

Grilled Chicken with Eggplant Salsa

Barbecued Chicken

Asian Pork with Hot Peanut Sauce

Steak Kebabs with Barbecue Sauce

Asian Spareribs

Sausage, Peppers and Onions

Mahimahi with Pineapple-Pepper Salsa

Marinated Sirloin and Onion Sandwiches

Grilled Flank Steak

Grilled Orange Salmon

Chicken and Fruit Kebabs

Jamaican Jerked Shrimp

| | |
|---|---|
| Hawaiian Chicken | Mexican Burgers |
| Marinated Filet Mignon of Tuna | Asian Turkey Burgers |
| Grilled Swordfish with Citrus Salsa | Tuna Steaks and Vegetable Kebabs |
| Grilled Chicken and Tomato Relish | Portobellos with Olive Oil, Shallots and Garlic |
| Grilled Scallop Kebabs | Grilled Corn and Pepper Relish |
| Grilled Pink Grapefruit and Pork Skewers | Grilled Vegetables with Toasts |
| Brazilian Marinated Steaks with Chili Lime Sauce | Summer Squash and Pepper Slaw |
| Steak Fajitas | Ham and Cheese Portobello Mushrooms |
| Grilled Peppers and Shrimp | Corn on the Cob with Basil Butter |
| Shish Kebabs | Curried Bananas |
| Vegetable Brochettes | Wine Spiced Peaches |
| Herbed Salmon Burgers | |

Here are my tips for the best barbecues or grilled dishes ever! First, I'll tell you about the two ways of cooking on a barbecue or outdoor grill. It pays to know the difference because you'll be able to choose the best cooking method for the recipe you're using.

There is direct cooking, which works about the same way as broiling; food is cooked directly over the heat source. It's the method most of us were familiar with until gas grills became so sophisticated and popular. Direct cooking is best for foods that take under a half hour to cook, or foods that benefit from searing to seal in the flavorful juices. Think steaks, chops, sausages and kebabs. If charcoal briquettes are used, the hot coals should be spread evenly over the cooking rack and the food centered above them.

Then there is indirect cooking. This method of cooking is somewhat similar to roasting. To be most successful, hot charcoal briquettes should be placed on either side of the food, or only the side burners of a gas grill should be on. The cover is completely closed on either a charcoal or gas grill so that heat reflects off the lid and circulates all around the food, much in the manner of a convection oven. I like this cooking method especially for large cuts of meat (after they have been seared on the sides), whole turkeys and chickens, roasts and ribs. When using the indirect method, I also find it helpful to place a drip pan under the roast to collect those delicious juices you can make into gravy later.

For a special flavor twist, I recommend adding hickory, mesquite or apple wood chips or chunks to the smoker box of your gas grill. Or simply place them on top of the hot coals if you're using traditional charcoal. Just be sure to soak them in water for 30 minutes before use. Either way, the fragrant wood will impart a distinctive taste to whatever food you're cooking.

I'm also a fan of rotisserie cooking. Many of the newer model gas grills and barbecue kettles have an optional attachment for just this purpose that turns automatically with no manual assistance required. With the rotisserie method, the meat or poultry slowly rotates during the cooking process so the juices are self-basting. The result is divinely succulent meat or poultry with tantalizingly crispy skin and pure eating pleasure, I think.

Along with all the sophisticated gas grills on the market and stovetop grills, I am always captivated by the latest grilling gadget, long-handled fork or skewer set. I know I don't have to have them all, but there are some indispensable tools I can't do without. For instance, I find an extra wide metal spatula with a long, heatproof, wooden handle essential for turning large pieces of meat and fish fillets. It works well and your fish won't break apart or slide through the rack into the fire. I also have a favorite long-handled basting brush with natural bristles so that I can reach in safely and apply another layer of sauce to whatever I'm cooking. Which brings up the need to always have two well-insulated and heat-resistant oven mitts on hand. Also, given the vagaries of barbecues and current concerns about food safety, I find a meat thermometer indispensable. Using one is the only dependable way to ensure that your foods are being cooked properly.

# Potato Skins with Bacon, Cheddar and Sour Cream

MAKES 8 POTATO HALVES

*ALTHOUGH THIS IS TRADITIONAL "BAR FOOD," making them at home on the grill is festive and both children and adults love to nibble on them. Try some crumbled, cooked hot sausage instead of bacon as a spicy alternative. They are no friend to dieters, but if served along with a salad or grilled vegetables, they can become a meal in themselves.*

|   |   |
|---|---|
| 4 | small potatoes |
| 8 | strips bacon, cooked, drained |
| 1½ | cups shredded Cheddar cheese |
| ½ | cup sour cream |
| ¼ | cup sliced green onions |

Bake the potatoes for 45 minutes in a preheated 425°F oven. When they are done, split them open to allow the steam to escape as they cool. Scoop out the insides and set aside for another use.

Place the potato skins, cut side down, on a very hot grill and close the lid. Cook for 2 to 4 minutes. Remove from the grill and crumble a strip of bacon into each potato half. Evenly distribute the cheese between the potatoes, return them to the grill right side up and close the lid. Cook for 4 to 5 minutes, until the cheese has melted. Remove from the grill.

Top each potato with a tablespoon of sour cream and then sprinkle with the green onions. Serve immediately.

# Zucchini Boats with Blue Cheese, Walnuts and Pears

MAKES ABOUT 18

*THIS IS VERY RICH, ELEGANT, grown-up fare. Other strong cheeses can be used instead of blue, but it must be one with a bit of a bite in order to balance the sweetness of the pears and the richness of the walnuts. This mixture also works well stuffed into mushroom caps.*

2 to 3 medium zucchini
½ cup coarsely chopped walnuts
½ cup peeled diced pears
¾ cup crumbled blue cheese

Trim the stem off each zucchini and halve lengthwise. Scoop out the seeds and cut into 3- to 4-inch lengths.

Place the hollowed-out boats flat side down on a grill that has been brought to a medium-high heat and cook until sear marks appear, about 2 to 4 minutes. Remove from the grill and evenly divide the walnuts and pears in the hollow of each boat. Sprinkle with the blue cheese and return them to the grill. Put the lid down and cook until the cheese melts, about 2 to 4 minutes.

# Grilled Chicken Wrapped with Green Onions

SERVES 4

*ALTHOUGH THIS RECIPE REQUIRES manual dexterity, it is well worth the effort. If you've never grilled green onions before you will soon discover just how fabulous they are. The barbecue mellows their oniony bite and makes them sweet and tender. The coarse salt heightens this flavor, making them irresistible.*

1½ pounds skinless boneless chicken breasts

½ cup soy sauce

2 tablespoons rice vinegar

2 tablespoons sugar

2 tablespoons sesame oil

3 garlic cloves, minced

2 bunches green onions

2 tablespoons coarse salt

½ cup soy sauce

2 green onions, sliced

1 tablespoon sesame oil

1 teaspoon sugar

Toothpicks

Cut the chicken into 1-inch cubes and place in a medium-size mixing bowl. In a small mixing bowl, combine the soy sauce, rice vinegar, 2 tablespoons sugar, 2 tablespoons sesame oil and garlic. Stir until the sugar is dissolved. Pour the marinade over the chicken and toss to coat all the cubes. Cover with plastic wrap and refrigerate for 1 hour. Stir once during that time.

Bring the grill to a medium-high heat and place the 2 bunches of green onions perpendicular to the grillwork. Sprinkle with 1 tablespoon of the coarse salt and close the lid of the grill. Cook for 2 to 3 minutes and, using long metal tongs, turn the green onions. Sprinkle with the remaining salt and cook for 1 to 2 minutes more. Remove from the grill.

Drain the chicken and place on the grill. Using long, metal tongs, turn the chicken as it begins to brown. Remove each piece as it becomes evenly browned, about 5 to 7 minutes. Stir together the soy sauce, sliced green onions, 1 tablespoon sesame oil and 1 teaspoon sugar. Pour into individual ramekins.

Assemble the chicken bites by wrapping each cube in a green onion. Secure with a toothpick. Warm in the oven just before serving. Serve with the dipping sauce.

# Bruschetta

*WHEN TOMATOES ARE AT THEIR PEAK, this is a quick and easy use for them. These little nibbles are fresh and healthy and the taste cannot be beat. Top with chopped fresh herbs, some slivers of black olives, or just some cracked black pepper.*

2 medium tomatoes, seeded, chopped

6 to 8 large garlic cloves, finely chopped

½ medium onion, finely chopped

6 ½-inch-thick slices French or Italian bread

Olive oil

In a medium bowl, combine the tomatoes, garlic and onion. Set aside.

Place the bread slices on the grill, flipping frequently so that both sides get browned, with a little char along the edges here and there.

Pull the bread off the grill, immediately brush with the olive oil, then top with the tomato, garlic and onion mixture. Serve immediately.

# Hot 'n Sassy Chicken Legs and Wings

MAKES ABOUT 20 PIECES

*CHILDREN AS WELL AS ADULTS adore these sweet and sticky legs and wings. Serve with some oven roasted potatoes and a tossed salad for a simple, flavorful meal, or serve alone on a platter as an appetizer.*

2 cups barbecue sauce

10 ounces spicy Dijon-style mustard

10 ounces honey

Hot pepper sauce (such as Tabasco) to taste

10 small chicken or cornish game hen legs

10 chicken wings, tips removed from joint

In a large bowl, combine the barbecue sauce, mustard, honey and hot pepper sauce. Bring the grill to a medium-high heat. Dip the legs into the barbecue sauce and cook for 5 to 7 minutes, turning as sear marks appear. Remove from the heat. Dip the wings into the barbecue sauce and shake off any excess. Place on the grill and cook for 4 to 5 minutes on each side. Remove and serve immediately.

# Grilled Chicken with Eggplant Salsa

SERVES 4

*MANY MIDDLE EASTERN SALSAS like this one are served with breads before a meal. Here it is paired with chicken, but it also goes well with steak or lamb. A dollop of tahini sauce or hummus can be added for richness.*

## SALSA

- 1   1-pound eggplant
- 1   tablespoon olive oil
- ½   cup chopped red onions
- 2   jalapeño peppers, seeded, chopped
- 2   garlic cloves, chopped
- 2   tablespoons chopped fresh basil
- 2   tablespoons chopped fresh cilantro
- 1   tablespoon chopped fresh mint
- 1   teaspoon sesame seeds, toasted
- 1   tablespoon fresh lime juice
- 1   teaspoon sugar
- ½   teaspoon sesame oil (hot if preferred)
      Salt and freshly ground pepper to taste

## VINAIGRETTE

- 2½   tablespoons balsamic vinegar
- 2   tablespoons chopped shallots
- 1   garlic clove, minced
- ½   teaspoon ground cumin
- 6   tablespoons olive oil
- 1   teaspoon chopped fresh basil
      Salt and freshly ground pepper to taste
- 4   skinless boneless chicken breasts
      Olive oil
- ¼   cup drained large capers

**FOR SALSA:** Char the eggplant under the broiler until blackened, about 12 minutes. Cool, then peel the skin from the eggplant. Cut eggplant into ¼-inch pieces and place on paper towels to drain. Heat the olive oil in a medium skillet over medium heat. Add the onions, jalapeños and garlic. Cook 5 minutes, covered, then stir in the basil, cilantro, mint and sesame seeds. Remove from the heat. Combine the lime juice, sugar and sesame oil in a medium bowl, then stir in the onion mixture. Mix in the eggplant and season with salt and pepper to taste. Let stand for 2 hours before using.

**FOR VINAIGRETTE:** Combine the vinegar, shallots, garlic and cumin in a small bowl. Gradually whisk in the oil, then stir in the basil. Season with salt and pepper. Cover and refrigerate until needed.

Season the chicken with salt and pepper, then brush with the oil. Grill over medium-high heat until cooked through, about 7 minutes per side. Slice and transfer to plates.

Warm the salsa in one saucepan and the vinaigrette in another. When warm, drizzle vinaigrette over the chicken and then spoon the salsa along the side. Sprinkle with capers and serve.

# Asian Pork with Hot Peanut Sauce

SERVES 4

*THE SMOKINESS OF THE BARBECUE combines beautifully with the richness of the peanut sauce, adding to the spicy flavors. If you can't find pork tenderloins, turkey tenders work well as a substitute. Serve this with white rice or cellophane noodles and some stir-fried vegetables for a complete Asian affair.*

| | |
|---|---|
| 4 | 10- to 12-ounce pork tenderloins |
| ½ | cup soy sauce |
| 3 | garlic cloves, minced |
| 1 | tablespoon freshly grated gingerroot |
| 1 | tablespoon sesame oil |
| ¼ | cup rice wine vinegar |
| ¼ | cup water |
| 2 | tablespoons sugar |
| 2 | tablespoons sliced green onion |
| 2 | garlic cloves, minced |
| 1 | tablespoon soy sauce |
| 2 | teaspoons sesame oil |
| ¼ | cup roasted unsalted peanuts |
| ¼ | cup chunky peanut butter |

Place the tenderloins in a 9 x 13-inch baking pan. Stir together the soy sauce, garlic, ginger and sesame oil. Pour over the pork, cover and refrigerate for 2 hours. Turn the pork 2 or 3 times while it marinates.

In a medium-size, heavy saucepot, bring the vinegar, water and sugar to a boil. When the sugar is dissolved, add the green onion, garlic, soy sauce and sesame oil and boil for 2 minutes. Remove from the heat.

In a food processor fitted with a metal blade, chop the peanuts until they are the size of the chunks in the peanut butter. Pour in the vinegar mixture and then add the peanut butter. Process until smooth. Pour back into the saucepot to reheat just before serving.

Bring the grill to a medium heat. Place the tenderloins on the grill and cook for 12 to 15 minutes. Roll the tenderloins every few minutes to brown evenly. Remove from the grill and let rest for 5 minutes before slicing.

Reheat the sauce and ladle a few tablespoons onto each plate. Slice the meat on the bias about ½-inch thick. Place the pork on top of the sauce in a shingled, semicircle shape.

# Asian Spareribs

*This is a great Asian sauce to have tucked away in your refrigerator. Keep it chilled in a tightly sealed container and it will last for up to three weeks. Marinate a steak with it or brush it on fish just before grilling and the flavors will form a delicate, sweet and spicy crust.*

½ cup soy sauce

⅓ cup dry Sherry

¼ cup vegetable oil

¼ cup sugar

2 large garlic cloves, minced

2 teaspoons freshly grated gingerroot or 1 teaspoon ground ginger

4 pounds baby back ribs

In a small bowl, whisk together all of the ingredients except for the ribs. Cover and let stand for at least 1 hour before using, to let the flavors blend.

Marinate the spareribs in the sauce for 2 to 3 hours before grilling. Bring the grill to a medium heat and cook the ribs for 45 minutes. Turn and baste often while cooking.

# Mahimahi with Pineapple-Pepper Salsa

MAKES 2 LARGE SERVINGS

*SAVE THIS FOR GUESTS WHO ENJOY experimenting with new flavors and are not afraid of a bit of spice. Serve with a rice pilaf tossed with pine nuts or currants and a crisp green vegetable. The combination of colors and flavors are perfect for a warm summer's evening dinner.*

1½ cups chopped fresh pineapple or 1 12- to 16-ounce can crushed in juice

1 small red bell pepper, coarsely chopped

½ cup chopped green onions

2 jalapeño peppers, seeded, chopped

3 tablespoons chopped fresh cilantro

1 tablespoon fresh lime juice

½ teaspoon salt

1 pound mahimahi fillets

1 tablespoon olive oil

¼ teaspoon cayenne pepper

¾ cup water

½ cup dry white wine

In a medium bowl, stir together the pineapple, bell pepper, green onions, jalapeños, cilantro, lime juice and ¼ teaspoon of the salt. Reserve at room temperature for about 1 hour.

Prepare the mahimahi by rubbing it with the oil and sprinkling it with the remaining salt and the cayenne. Place it in a steaming pan with the water and white wine. Place the pan on the grill over a medium-hot fire and cook for 8 to 10 minutes or until the fish is just flaking apart.

Serve with the salsa spooned on top.

# Grilled Flank Steak

SERVES 6

*FLANK STEAK IS A FLAVORFUL CUT which lends itself well to grilling. It is slightly thicker on one end, so you will be able to serve your guests medium-rare and medium-well-done meat without any fuss.*

1  3-pound flank steak

3  garlic cloves, minced

1  tablespoon freshly grated gingerroot

⅓  cup soy sauce

2  tablespoons sesame oil

Place the steak on a large enough plate or shallow pan so that it lies flat. Combine the remaining ingredients and pour the mixture over the meat. Turn the meat a few times so that it has been completely coated. Cover with plastic wrap and refrigerate for up to 1 hour. Halfway through the marinating time, turn the meat to the other side.

Bring the grill to a high heat. Place the meat over the fire and cook for 5 to 7 minutes on each side or until cooked to desired doneness. Allow the meat to rest for 10 minutes before slicing.

Cut the meat thinly, across the grain and on an angle, and serve.

# Chicken and Fruit Kebabs

SERVES 4

*IF YOU'VE SEEN STAR FRUIT in the grocery store but never knew just what to do with them, here's your chance. They may look awfully exotic, but in fact they are simple, attractive and delicious. Serve along with some white rice or Asian noodles.*

8   10-inch wooden skewers

1   pound skinless boneless chicken breasts

1   cup cubed fresh pineapple

1   pint cherry tomatoes

8   green onions

¼   cup fresh lemon juice

¼   cup Dijon-style mustard

2   tablespoons olive oil

1   tablespoon sugar

1   tablespoon crushed black pepper

1   teaspoon salt

4   ripe peaches

4   star fruit

¼   cup fresh lemon juice

½   cup balsamic vinegar

4   tablespoons unsalted butter, softened

Place the skewers in a shallow pan and cover with water. Cut the chicken breasts into 2-inch cubes and place in a large bowl. Add the pineapple, cherry tomatoes and green onions.

Whisk together the lemon juice, mustard, olive oil, sugar, pepper and salt. Pour over the chicken mixture and toss well. Cover and refrigerate for ½ hour. Stir every 10 minutes.

While the grill is heating up, assemble the kebabs. Divide the chicken, pineapple, tomatoes and green onions evenly and pierce with the skewers. Fold the green onions so they won't stick out too much.

Place the kebabs on the grill over medium-high heat and cook for 7 to 10 minutes. Turn as each side becomes seared.

Peel, halve and pit the peaches. Cut the star fruit into ½-inch slices. Place the peaches and star fruit in a bowl and toss with the lemon juice. Place the fruit on the grill and cook until sear marks appear. Turn the fruit over and cook until warmed through.

In a small, heavy saucepot, bring the balsamic vinegar to a rolling boil. Turn off the heat and add the butter, 1 tablespoon at a time. Swirl the butter and vinegar until each lump melts before adding the next.

Pour the balsamic sauce on the bottom of each plate and place the peach and star fruit on top. Place 2 kebabs on each plate alongside the fruit and sauce.

# Summer's Best Pizza

SERVES 4

*Barbecued pizza? Yes and it's fun to make! Kids enjoy helping with the punching, kneading and stretching process and each person can personalize their own pizza by selecting what goes on top. Improvise with the suggested ingredient list here and enjoy the amazing flavor of grilled pizza.*

1   cup warm water
1   1¼-ounce package active dry yeast
    Pinch white sugar
1   teaspoon salt
1   tablespoon olive oil
3   cups all-purpose flour
2   garlic cloves, minced
2   tablespoons chopped fresh basil
⅓   cup olive oil
4   tablespoons tomato sauce
1   cup chopped tomatoes
¼   cup chopped fresh basil
½   cup diced yellow bell peppers
2   cups grated smoked mozzarella cheese

In a medium-size bowl, stir together the warm water and yeast. Add the sugar and place in a warm spot to proof for 10 minutes. Stir down the foamy mixture and add the salt, olive oil and flour. Mix until the dough begins to pull away from the sides of the bowl. Turn onto a lightly floured board and knead for 8 to 10 minutes, until it is smooth and stretchy. You may need to sprinkle with some more flour as you are working. Place the dough in a well-oiled bowl and turn until the dough is coated. Cover with a damp cloth, set aside in a warm spot and let rise until doubled in size, about 1 hour.

Punch down the dough and turn onto a lightly floured board. Sprinkle with the minced garlic and fresh basil and knead until they are incorporated into the dough. Cover and set aside for another ½ hour. Bring the grill to a medium-high heat.

Punch down the dough and divide in half. Place both pieces on a lightly floured sheet pan and stretch each piece into an oblong shape at about ½-inch thickness. Brush the grill with olive oil. Place the 2 pieces of dough on the grill and cook for 3 to 5 minutes, until the bottoms begin to brown. Using 2 spatulas, flip each piece over and brush with olive oil. Spoon 2 tablespoons of tomato sauce over each pizza. Sprinkle both evenly with the tomatoes, basil, yellow peppers and smoked mozzarella. Put the lid of the grill down and cook until the cheese has melted and the other ingredients begin to bubble, about 5 minutes.

# Grilled Sweet and Spicy Salmon

SERVES 4

*If GRILLING FISH SEEMS too intimidating to you, give this a try. Salmon is a firm fish that will not fall apart very easily, and since the skin remains on during the first half of the cooking, it is that much more stable. The honey in the sauce helps to prevent it from sticking.*

1  3-pound salmon fillet

2  tablespoons Dijon-style mustard

¼  cup honey

Cut the salmon into 4 pieces, leaving the skin on. Combine the mustard and honey. Place the salmon on the grill over a high heat, skin side down. Brush the top with the mustard mixture.

When the bottom third of the salmon turns opaque, about 3 to 5 minutes, turn the salmon over. The skin may stick to the grill. Scrape it off with a metal spatula. If the skin does not come off, slip a knife under it and slide it off. Scrape off any dark gray flesh.

Brush with more mustard sauce and cook until the bottom third is opaque, about 2 to 3 minutes. Remove from the grill and serve immediately, skin side down, with extra mustard sauce on the side.

# Steak with Chimichurri Sauce

SERVES 4

*PITY THE POOR MASTER of the barbecue grill! He's got to make sure that everybody's steak comes out just the way they want it, and all at the same time. It truly is an art—if you don't have some tricks up your sleeve. Like this recipe for instance. A flank steak is tapered, so the thinner end of the steak will be well-done while the thicker middle sections are medium or medium-rare. That way, everybody gets what they want, and you cook it once without worrying about it. And I guarantee everyone will love the sauce.*

1½ pounds flank steak

4 garlic cloves, finely chopped

1 cup vegetable oil

½ cup white wine vinegar

½ cup fresh lemon juice

¼ cup snipped fresh parsley

1 teaspoon crushed red pepper

Cut a diamond pattern ⅛-inch deep into both sides of the beef. Place the beef in a shallow glass pan or plastic dish so it lies flat. Shake the remaining ingredients in a tightly covered jar. Pour 1 cup of the sauce over the beef. Cover the remaining sauce and set aside. Cover and refrigerate the beef, turning occasionally, for at least 4 hours.

Remove the beef from the sauce. Grill the beef 4 or 5 inches from the fire, turning and brushing with the remaining sauce once, until desired doneness—6 to 8 minutes on each side for medium-rare. Cut the beef diagonally across the grain into thin slices. Serve with the reserved sauce.

# Moroccan Leg of Lamb

SERVES 8 TO 10

*THIS IS A GREAT RECIPE for feeding a crowd. It's easy and full of flavors that compliment even the simplest side dishes of rice, potatoes or vegetables. It is great hot off the grill or made into sandwiches the next day.*

1   medium red onion, chopped

6   garlic cloves

½   cup olive oil

2   tablespoons fresh lemon juice

2   tablespoons fresh lime juice

2   teaspoons ground cumin

2   teaspoons paprika

1   teaspoon cayenne pepper

1   teaspoon ground coriander

1   teaspoon salt

1   teaspoon freshly ground pepper

½   cup chopped fresh cilantro

1   8- to 8½-pound leg of lamb, boned, butterflied

Place all of the ingredients except the lamb into the bowl of a food processor fitted with a metal blade. Chop until it forms a paste. Place the lamb in a large glass or porcelain pan (aluminum will react with the lime and lemon juice). Smear both sides of the meat with the onion paste. Cover with plastic wrap and refrigerate for 3 to 10 hours.

Bring the grill to a medium-high heat. Place the meat on the grill and cook for 10 to 12 minutes on each side or until the thickest part of the meat is medium-rare (140°F). Remove the meat from the grill and let it rest for 10 minutes before slicing.

# Cilantro Shrimp

*IN THE HEAT OF THE SUMMER, this is a wonderful, light meal. Other fresh seafoods like scallops or squid can be added to the shrimp. The flavors are great straight from the grill, at room temperature or even chilled.*

| | |
|---|---|
| 2 | tablespoons fresh lime juice |
| 2 | tablespoons olive oil |
| 3 | garlic cloves, minced |
| ½ | teaspoon salt |
| ½ | teaspoon freshly ground pepper |
| 2 | pounds medium shrimp, peeled deveined |
| 10 | 10-inch wooden skewers |
| ½ | yellow bell pepper, seeded |
| ¼ | cup finely chopped fresh cilantro |

In a medium-size mixing bowl, whisk together the lime juice, olive oil, garlic, salt and pepper. Add the shrimp and toss to coat. Cover with plastic wrap and refrigerate for 2 hours.

While the grill is heating up, put the shrimp on the skewers. When the grill is hot, place the yellow pepper and the shrimp in the center of the grill. Cook for about 2 or 3 minutes and then turn both the shrimp and the pepper. Cook for another 2 to 3 minutes and remove from the heat.

Slip the shrimp off the skewers into a medium-size mixing bowl. Dice the yellow peppers and add to the shrimp. Sprinkle with the cilantro and toss well. Serve immediately over rice or pasta.

# Barbecued Chicken

SERVES 4

*THE KEY TO JUICY, FLAVORFUL barbecued chicken without the overwhelming flavor of char is to cook it in stages. It is easier and neater than soaking the chicken in sauce and trying to see through the glaze to tell if the meat is done cooking.*

1  3- to 5- pound chicken, quartered

1  pint barbecue sauce

½  cup maple syrup

1  tablespoon dry mustard

Bring the grill to a medium-high heat. Place the chicken on the grill and cook for 7 to 10 minutes. Halfway through, turn each piece over.

Keep an eye on the meat since the fat under the skin will melt and cause the fire to flame-up. If this happens, just move the piece of chicken to another part of the grill surface. You may need to do this several times.

After each piece of chicken is nicely browned and cooked about halfway through, remove them from the grill. Let the meat rest for 5 to 10 minutes. In a small bowl, whisk together the barbecue sauce, maple syrup and dry mustard. Use this time to prepare other parts of the meal that will accompany the chicken.

Brush each piece of chicken with the sauce and return it, sauce side down, to the grill. Cook on one side for 5 minutes. Just before turning to the other side, brush it with sauce and then cook the other side for 5 more minutes.

Cut a small slit in a leg or thigh piece and peek in to see if the flesh is too pink. Be careful not to make too big a cut in the meat, as that will cause the juices to flow out. If the chicken is underdone, allow the chicken to stay on the grill, or you can transfer it to a 350°F oven.

This technique will allow for flavorful barbecued chicken that is not blackened by char but maintains its outdoor, grilled flavor.

# Steak Kebabs with Barbecue Sauce

SERVES 2

*KEBABS, SERVED WITH A RICH SAUCE like this one, are wonderful over rice. The sauce can be made a few days in advance and kept in the refrigerator, making this an easy dinner to pull together at the end of the day. Vegetables like onions, peppers or cherry tomatoes can be added to the skewers to round out the meal.*

**SAUCE**

  2  tablespoons vegetable oil

  1  large onion, finely minced

  4  large garlic cloves, finely minced

  4  cups ketchup

  ¾  cup cider vinegar

  ¾  cup firmly packed dark brown sugar

  ¼  cup dark molasses

  2  tablespoons dry mustard

2½  teaspoons cayenne pepper

  1  teaspoon ground white pepper

  2  teaspoons chili powder

  ¼  cup Worcestershire sauce

1½  teaspoons ground cumin

**KEBABS**

  1  7- to 8-ounce strip steak, cut into 1-inch cubes

  4  8-inch bamboo skewers

**FOR SAUCE:** In a 3-quart saucepan, place the oil, onion and garlic. Cook over medium heat, stirring often, for 5 minutes. Do not let the onion brown.

Add the remaining ingredients for the sauce and stir well. Heat slowly, then simmer for about 30 minutes over low heat. (The sauce can be used hot or cold with a variety of meats.)

**FOR KEBABS:** Place the skewers in a shallow pan and cover with water. Soak for at least 15 minutes. Thread the steak cubes onto the skewers and place on the grill. Grill the kebabs, turning as sear marks appear, over medium-high heat for 8 to 10 minutes. Top with the sauce when done.

# Sausage, Peppers and Onions

SERVES 4

*Now is the time to try all the different types of sausage you've seen in the butcher's meat case. Buy a variety and slice them into 1-inch, bias cut pieces so that each person can sample a range of flavors, or select just the kind they prefer.*

3 pounds sweet or hot Italian sausage or sausage of your choice

2 large white onions

2 large green bell peppers

½ cup olive oil

1 teaspoon garlic powder

Bring the grill to a medium-high heat. In a large pot of simmering water, blanch the sausage for 5 to 7 minutes. Drain and set aside.

Peel and halve the onions. Halve, core and seed the green peppers. In a small mixing bowl, stir together the olive oil and garlic powder. Brush onto the onions and peppers.

Place the sausage and peppers in the center of the grill and the onions around the side. Put the lid down and cook for 3 to 4 minutes, then turn the sausage, peppers and onions over. Brush again with the olive oil mixture. Cook for another 5 minutes with the lid down. Remove the peppers and set aside. Cook until the sausage is browned all over. Remove the sausage and onions. When cool enough to handle, slice the sausage on the bias, 1-inch thick. Slice the peppers lengthwise and the onions into ¼-inch slices.

# Marinated Sirloin and Onion Sandwiches

MAKES 4 SANDWICHES

*HERE ARE COLORFUL AND HEARTY sandwiches that will satisfy even the most hungry. Be sure to slice the meat into very thin slices so it's not too difficult to eat. A sourdough, French-style bread is particularly good here.*

1½  pounds 2-inch-thick sirloin steak

½  cup red wine vinegar

⅓  cup dry red wine

2  tablespoons olive oil

4  garlic cloves, minced

2  tablespoons chopped fresh rosemary

1  teaspoon salt

1  teaspoon freshly ground pepper

1  red onion

2  red bell peppers

Olive oil

1  loaf crusty French bread

½  cup chopped fresh basil

Place the steak in a small, shallow baking pan. Whisk together the vinegar, wine, olive oil, garlic, rosemary, salt and pepper. Pour over the steak. Cover with plastic wrap and refrigerate for 2 to 6 hours. Flip the steak over every half hour.

Bring the grill to a high heat and cook the steak for 6 to 8 minutes per side for medium-rare. Remove to a cutting board and allow to rest for at least 10 minutes.

While the steak is resting, peel and cut the onion into ½-inch-thick slices. Cut the peppers in half and remove the seeds. Brush both with olive oil and grill until sear marks appear. Turn and cook on the other side. Remove.

Cut the bread into 6-inch pieces and halve lengthwise. Brush the insides with olive oil and place on the grill until it is nicely toasted.

To assemble the sandwiches, cut the steak on the bias into thin strips. Place the meat on the bottom half of the bread. Loosen the onions into rings and place over the meat. Cut the peppers into 1-inch-thick strips and place half a pepper on each sandwich. Sprinkle with the basil and cover with the remaining bread.

# Grilled Orange Salmon

SERVES 4

*BOTTLED BARBECUE SAUCE IS OFTEN a great base for your own personal creation. Here is an example that is rich and full-flavored. It goes well with salmon or any other firm steak cut of fish.*

1   10-ounce bottle hickory barbecue sauce

½   cup frozen orange juice concentrate (no water added)

3   tablespoons soy sauce

2   tablespoons Dijon-style mustard

2   tablespoons dry Sherry

4   teaspoons finely chopped gingerroot

3   garlic cloves, minced

1   tablespoon red wine vinegar

1   to 2 tablespoons brown sugar

2   teaspoons hot sesame oil

4   ½-pound salmon steaks

In a blender, combine the barbecue sauce, orange juice concentrate, soy sauce, mustard, Sherry, ginger, garlic, vinegar, brown sugar and sesame oil. Liquify or puree until a smooth liquid is formed. Place the salmon steaks in an oblong baking dish and pour the marinade over the top. Let stand for about 1 hour.

Bring the grill to a medium-high heat. Gently lift the salmon steaks from the marinade and place on the grill rack. Cover and grill, turning the steaks 2 to 3 times (baste with the marinade after each time that you turn them).

The salmon is done when it is starting to flake easily, and is well glazed and lightly brown. Grill for a total of about 9 to 10 minutes for medium.

# Jamaican Jerked Shrimp

*"CURRY" IS A TERM USED IN INDIAN CUISINE for a spice mixture. A "rub" is what it is often called in other cuisines, including Caribbean. It is a dry marinade for meats and can become as personalized as you'd like. Increase or decrease the spices according to your own preferences. Serve this recipe along with some rice and chutney for a main course, or with a yogurt cucumber dipping sauce as an appetizer.*

In a small mixing bowl, combine all the seasonings and the oil. Place the shrimp in a medium-size mixing bowl and toss with the spice rub until they are all well coated. Bring the grill to a high heat and cook the shrimp for 2 to 4 minutes per side. Remove from the heat and serve immediately.

| | |
|---|---|
| 1 | teaspoon thyme |
| ¼ | teaspoon salt |
| 1 | teaspoon curry powder |
| ¼ | teaspoon sugar |
| ¾ | teaspoon sage |
| ¼ | teaspoon cayenne pepper |
| ¾ | teaspoon ground allspice |
| ½ | teaspoon paprika |
| ¼ | teaspoon ground cinnamon |
| ¼ | teaspoon ground nutmeg |
| ⅛ | teaspoon ground cloves |
| 1 | large garlic clove, minced |
| 2 | teaspoons canola oil |
| 1 | dozen large shrimp, peeled, deveined |

# Hawaiian Chicken

SERVES 3

*MANY SOUTH PACIFIC RECIPES use pineapple as a tenderizer and flavor enhancer. It is wonderful for chicken and many firm fish. Be sure not to marinate too long as the acids in the pineapple juice are powerful and will cause the meat or fish to become too soft.*

½  cup drained fresh pineapple chunks

⅓  cup canned coconut milk

1  2-inch piece gingerroot, peeled, thinly sliced

¼  teaspoon salt

¼  teaspoon freshly ground pepper

3  skinless boneless chicken breasts

In a blender, combine the pineapple, coconut milk, ginger, salt and pepper and process until smooth.

Place the chicken breasts in a shallow dish, top with the pineapple mixture, cover and let marinate for 2 to 3 hours in the fridge.

Bring the grill to a medium-high heat. Place the chicken on the grill, reserving the marinade for basting, and grill for 6 to 8 minutes on each side. Brush with the marinade often. Serve immediately (do not use the marinade again after cooking!).

# Marinated Filet Mignon of Tuna

SERVES 4

*GINGER IS AT ITS MOST FULL FLAVORED and tender in the spring. Be sure to peel it over the mixing bowl so that all the juices are captured. In this recipe, the tuna will soak up the zesty, fresh flavor of ginger.*

**MARINADE**

- 2 cups teriyaki sauce
- ½ cup dry Sherry
- 4 tablespoons peeled finely chopped gingerroot
- ½ cup chopped green onions
- 2 garlic cloves, thinly sliced
- ½ teaspoon cayenne pepper
- 2 teaspoons freshly ground pepper
- Juice of 2 lemons

**TUNA**

- 4 8- to 10-ounce yellowfin tuna steaks, cut into 3-inch cubes
- 2 tablespoons olive oil
- ¼ cup freshly minced gingerroot

**F**OR MARINADE: Combine all of the marinade ingredients in a bowl large enough to hold the tuna and mix well.

**FOR TUNA:** Place the tuna cubes in the marinade and refrigerate for 3 hours, turning every hour. Thirty minutes before cooking, drain the tuna and bring to room temperature. Bring the grill to a very high heat.

Brush the tuna with the olive oil. Grill the cubes for 1 to 2 minutes on each of their 6 sides. The outside of the tuna should be nicely charred and the center should be barely warm and quite rare.

Cooked this way, the tuna will remain moist and flavorful. Top each steak with the minced ginger and serve.

# Grilled Swordfish with Citrus Salsa

SERVES 2

*SINCE THIS IS SUCH A BEAUTIFULLY colored salsa, it looks and tastes great served over a bed of white rice. The juices are absorbed by the rice and all the flavors are saved to be enjoyed! Pair this with a simple, tossed green salad for a healthy, low-fat dinner.*

1   small red onion, chopped

1   garlic clove, minced

1   chili pepper, peeled, seeded,
    coarsely chopped

1   tablespoon olive oil

3   tablespoons fresh lime juice

2   tablespoons chopped fresh cilantro
    Salt and freshly ground pepper to taste

2   1-inch-thick swordfish steaks,
    cut into 1-inch cubes

2   medium oranges, peeled, pith and
    seeds removed, divided into sections
    Olive oil

In the bowl of a food processor or blender, process the onion, garlic, chili pepper, olive oil, lime juice, cilantro, salt and pepper, pulsing and scraping the sides to make sure all the ingredients are blended. Add the oranges and continue to process until you have a chunky, well-combined mixture. Set aside.

Brush the swordfish with the olive oil and sprinkle with salt and pepper to taste. Bring the grill to a high heat and place the swordfish cubes on the grill. Sear on each of the 6 sides, 3 to 4 minutes per side, until the fish is firm but still springs back when pressed with a spatula. Serve immediately with the salsa by placing the swordfish cubes in a circle and spooning the salsa into the center.

# Grilled Chicken and Tomato Relish

SERVES 2

*WHEN TOMATOES ARE AT THEIR PEAK, try adding some of the yellow varietal tomatoes that are available to brighten this salsa. Serve with rice or noodles so that all the flavors are absorbed. Fish fillets can be used in place of the chicken.*

2  tablespoons olive oil

2  7- to 8-ounce boneless skinless chicken breasts

1  medium onion, chopped

1  garlic clove, minced

2  tablespoons dried basil or ¼ cup chopped fresh

3  medium pear tomatoes, cut in half lengthwise

Pound the breasts between pieces of wax paper if they are thick—they shouldn't be any fatter than about ½ inch. Rub the chicken breasts with 1 tablespoon of the olive oil and place on the grill over a medium-high heat. Cook for 4 to 6 minutes on each side.

Meanwhile, combine the remaining 1 tablespoon of oil, the onion and garlic in a large frying pan over medium heat. Cook, stirring often, until the onion is limp and golden. Stir in the basil. Stir in the tomatoes and cook until just limp.

Place the chicken breasts on a plate and surround with the tomato relish mixture.

# Grilled Scallop Kebabs

SERVES 2

*ALABTHOUGH IT IS ALWAYS BEST to opt for fresh, not frozen seafood, here is a recipe that will be terrific even with scallops that have been frozen. The lively flavors of the marinade are picked up by the scallops like a sponge. Serve this with rice and maybe a dollop of mango chutney as an accompaniment.*

¼ cup white wine vinegar
¼ cup dry Sherry
2 teaspoons chopped fresh thyme
4 thin slices gingerroot
2 jalapeño peppers, seeded, chopped
2 large garlic cloves, minced
½ teaspoon salt
¾ tablespoon olive oil
1 pound sea scallops
4 10-inch wooden skewers
1 red onion, cut into wide wedges
1 red bell pepper, cut into 1-inch squares

Prepare a grill by oiling the grill rack. In a long, shallow dish, combine the vinegar, Sherry, thyme, ginger, jalapeños, garlic, salt and oil. Place the scallops in the marinade, turning to coat. Let stand for about 1 hour, turning frequently.

Soak the skewers in water for 15 minutes. Thread the scallops onto the skewers, alternating with the onion and pepper squares. Baste with the marinade, then place the skewers over a high heat on a preheated grill. Cook the scallops, turning every few minutes, until they are firm but not rubbery, about 6 to 8 minutes. In a small pot, bring the remaining marinade to a boil and cook for 3 minutes. Strain and serve the skewers with the marinade as a dipping sauce.

# Grilled Pink Grapefruit and Pork Skewers

SERVES 2

*PINK GRAPEFRUIT IS SWEETER than its white cousin but still has a tartness that will enhance the flavor of grilled pork. The fresh ginger and lemon juice in the marinade is pungent and refreshing. The juices will permeate the meat giving it flavor as well as tenderizing it.*

1 whole ¾-pound pork tenderloin

¼ cup soy sauce

¼ cup firmly packed dark brown sugar

¼ cup fresh lemon juice

2 tablespoons dry Sherry

1 tablespoon freshly grated gingerroot

1 garlic clove, minced

1 pink grapefruit

4 10-inch wooden skewers

Cut the pork into 1-inch cubes and place in a bowl. Combine the remaining ingredients, except the grapefruit, and pour them over the pork. Cover and marinate for about 1 hour.

Slice the unpeeled grapefruit into 12 sections and halve each section.

Soak the skewers in water for 15 minutes. Thread the pork cubes alternately with the grapefruit pieces (piercing them through the peel) onto the wooden skewers. Reserve the marinade.

Bring the grill to a high heat and place the skewers on the grill. Turn and baste with the marinade, until cooked through thoroughly, about 15 minutes. Serve hot.

# Brazilian Marinated Steaks with Chili Lime Sauce

SERVES 4

*THIS STEAK IS NOT FOR THE FAINT OF HEART. Serve it to guests who enjoy a spicy sauce and be sure to provide cold beer and bread to mellow the flavors. Black beans and rice make a great, traditional accompaniment for this steak.*

## CHILI LIME SAUCE

- 5 to 10 malgueta or jalapeño peppers
- 1 teaspoon salt
- 1 small white onion, finely diced
- 4 large garlic cloves, chopped
  Juice of 3 limes
- ½ bunch Italian parsley (leaves only), chopped

## STEAKS

- 4 1½-inch-thick sirloin steaks
- ½ cup fresh lime juice
- ⅓ cup dry red wine
- 1 small onion, finely chopped
- 4 garlic cloves, finely chopped
- 2 teaspoons oregano
- 1 bay leaf
- 1 teaspoon coarse salt
- 1 teaspoon freshly ground pepper

**FOR LIME SAUCE:** Combine all of the ingredients in a mini-chopper or blender and grind or blend until a paste is formed. Set aside.

**FOR STEAKS:** Place the steaks in a single layer in a large glass or ceramic baking dish. Whisk the remaining ingredients for the steak together in a bowl and pour over the steaks, turning to coat evenly. Cover and refrigerate for about 4 hours, turning every couple of hours.

Bring the grill to a medium-high heat. Thirty minutes before cooking, drain the steaks and bring them to room temperature. Grill the steaks 6 to 8 minutes per side for medium-rare, or until done to taste.

Transfer to a platter and let the meat rest, loosely covered with foil. Serve with the chile lime sauce.

# Steak Fajitas

SERVES 5 TO 6

*OH, THE AROMA OF GRILLING PEPPERS AND ONIONS! Steak prepared in this manner is a hit with just about everybody. Chicken can be added to this marinade for a similar, but slightly lighter twist to the recipe. The pleasure of assembling each fajita is a taste challenge for each of your guests, so be sure to supply plenty of choices—guacamole, chopped cilantro, and sour cream to name a few—for the garnishes.*

| | |
|---|---|
| ⅓ | cup tequila |
| ¼ | cup fresh lime juice |
| 2 | tablespoons olive oil |
| 2 | garlic cloves, minced |
| ½ | teaspoon salt |
| ⅓ | teaspoon red pepper flakes |
| 2 | pounds sirloin or strip steak, fat trimmed |
| 2 | tablespoons olive oil |
| 2 | red onions, cut crosswise into ½-inch thick slices |
| 1 | red bell pepper, cut into ½-inch thick rings |
| 1 | green bell pepper, cut into ½-inch thick rings |
| | 8- to 10-inch flour tortillas steamed or warmed |
| | Guacamole |
| | Sour cream |

In a small bowl, whisk together the tequila, lime juice, oil, garlic, salt and pepper flakes. Place the steak in the bowl and turn several times to make sure it's coated. Let sit at least 3 hours to marinate.

Bring the grill to a medium-high heat; place the rack about 5 inches from the fire. Place the steak on the grill and cook for 5 to 7 minutes per side for medium-rare. Add the onions and peppers and grill until limp and slightly browned.

To serve, cut the steak into thin slices across the grain. Mound the steak slices on a platter and surround with the grilled onions and peppers. Serve with the warm tortillas, guacamole and sour cream. Each diner can place several pieces of steak on a tortilla and top with the onions and peppers. Add a dollop of guacamole or sour cream, roll up and enjoy.

# Grilled Peppers and Shrimp

SERVES 2

*WHEN BUYING SHRIMP for a recipe like this one where the flavor is not masked by a heavy sauce, it is best to always choose the fresh, not the frozen variety. They may be hard to locate, but their delicate taste will carry the day. A good, extra-virgin olive oil is also a good choice here as the subtle, fruity flavors will enhance the entire dish.*

8 to 10 extra large uncooked shrimp, peeled, deveined

2 tablespoons olive oil

1 garlic clove, minced

1 medium shallot, minced

½ teaspoon basil

½ large red bell pepper, seeded, cut into 1-inch squares

½ large yellow bell pepper, seeded, cut into 1-inch squares

½ large yellow squash, cut into ¼-inch-thick rounds, then halved

Place the shrimp in a bowl with the olive oil, garlic, shallot and basil. Toss to coat thoroughly. Let stand in the refrigerator for about 1 hour.

Bring the grill to a high heat. Set the pepper and squash pieces onto the grill, then place the shrimp onto the grill. Turn both after about 1 minute. Turn again as needed to grill thoroughly.

Place the shrimp in a fan shape in the center of a large serving dish and surround with the peppers and squash. Serve immediately.

# Shish Kebabs

Serves 4

*Even people who are reluctant to eat lamb will enjoy these kebabs. Vary them with shrimp or chicken kebabs and you will be sure to have something for everyone. Served over rice with some chopped, fresh green onions, they make a colorful presentation on a platter or individual plates.*

¼ cup olive oil

¼ cup soy sauce

Freshly ground pepper to taste

4 garlic cloves, minced

2 pounds lamb, cut into
1- to 1½-inch cubes

8 10-inch wooden skewers

2 large red onions, cut into
1½-inch sections

2 large green bell peppers, cut into
1½-inch sections

1 pound small to medium mushrooms

1 pound small cherry tomatoes

Combine the oil, soy sauce, pepper and garlic in a large bowl, then add the lamb and mix until coated well. Marinate for 2 to 3 hours.

Prepare the skewers by soaking them in water for 15 minutes. Alternate each of the remaining ingredients and the lamb on a skewer, but make sure you begin and end each skewer with a piece of lamb. Bring the grill to a medium-high heat and cook the kebabs for 8 to 10 minutes, until cooked through. Serve hot.

# Vegetable Brochettes

SERVES 4

*BUTTERNUT SQUASH IS SOMETIMES forgotten about in the summer as we often only eat it mashed or as a soup in the winter. It is sturdy and rich enough to replace meat in a meal. Serve this as a main course or side dish with a simple grilled steak or fish.*

| | |
|---|---|
| 1 | small butternut squash, peeled, seeded, cut into approximately 16 large chunks |
| 1 | 8-ounce can tomato sauce |
| 3 | garlic cloves, minced |
| 2 | tablespoons chopped fresh basil |
| 2 | teaspoons balsamic vinegar |
| ¾ | teaspoon ground ginger |
| ¼ | teaspoon salt or to taste |
| 8 | 10-inch wooden skewers |
| 1 | zucchini, cut into 16 rounds |
| 1 | yellow bell pepper, seeded, cut into 16 pieces |
| 1 | red bell pepper, seeded, cut into 16 pieces |
| 16 | medium mushrooms, stems removed |

In a large pot of boiling water, cook the squash for 15 minutes or until just about tender when poked with a fork, then drain.

Meanwhile, in a small bowl, combine the tomato sauce, garlic, basil, vinegar, ginger and salt. Set this mixture aside.

Soak the skewers in water for 15 minutes. Thread the vegetables onto the skewers, putting 2 pieces of each vegetable onto each skewer and alternating each kind. Bring the grill to a medium-high heat. Coat the vegetables well with the sauce, then place the skewers on the grill. Baste often during grilling when you turn them. They should be done in about 10 minutes, but don't let them burn.

# Herbed Salmon Burgers

SERVES 4

*FORTUNATELY YOU DON'T HAVE to confine your non-meat-eating guests to munching on veggies. These burgers are slightly more complex than regular hamburgers but are worth the effort for their healthiness and flavor. If you want to use fresh salmon, just poach it, cool and use as you would the canned fish.*

2   medium potatoes

1   tablespoon fresh lemon juice

2   tablespoons chopped fresh dill

2   tablespoons chopped fresh parsley

12  ounces cooked fresh salmon or
    canned

1   egg

1   egg white

Bring a medium pot of water to a boil. Peel and cube the potatoes. Simmer the potatoes until tender, about 20 minutes. Drain, place in a medium mixing bowl and mash with a fork.

Add the lemon juice, dill, parsley and salmon. Mix well.

In a small mixing bowl, whisk the egg and egg white until foamy. Add to the salmon mixture and fold until combined.

Form the mixture into 4 patties, cover with plastic wrap and refrigerate for ½ hour.

Bring the grill to a medium-high heat. Place the salmon patties on the grill and cook for 5 minutes on each side. Serve on white toast or other light bread.

# Mexican Burgers

*THESE BURGERS SHOULD CARRY a warning label on them for your guests! For anyone who likes their food spicy, these will be a new-found favorite. Of course, tone down the amount of jalapeño pepper and chili powder if you feel that it won't be appreciated by your crowd.*

1½  pounds ground beef

2  teaspoons chili powder

1  teaspoon ground cumin

1  jalapeño pepper, seeded

½  red onion

4  hamburger buns, toasted, or flour tortillas, warmed

1  cup salsa

½  cup sour cream

In a medium mixing bowl, combine the beef, chili powder and cumin. Mix well.

Finely dice the jalapeño pepper and onion and mix into the beef.

Form into 4 patties, cover with plastic wrap and refrigerate for ½ hour.

Bring the grill to a medium-high heat and place the meat on the grill. Cook for 8 to 10 minutes, turning once during that time.

Serve on toasted buns or warmed flour tortillas topped with salsa and a dollop of sour cream.

# Asian Turkey Burgers

*MANY OF US WHO ARE TRYING to stay away from red meat have discovered the versatility of ground turkey. But if you're not being a purist, a mixture of ground meats can be almost just as healthy while giving you a taste of some favorite forbidden foods like sausage, veal or even chopped bacon. This recipe is a good one to experiment with.*

1½   pounds ground turkey

1   tablespoon freshly grated gingerroot

1   tablespoon hoisin sauce

1   tablespoon soy sauce

2   teaspoons sesame oil

1   green onion, minced

½   teaspoon freshly ground pepper

4   sesame hamburger buns or large pita pockets

In a medium bowl, combine all of the ingredients, except for the bread, and mix well. Form into 4 patties, cover with plastic wrap and refrigerate for ½ hour.

Bring the grill to a medium-high heat and brush it lightly with oil. Place the burgers on the grill and cook for 8 to 10 minutes. Turn once during that time.

Serve on sesame seed hamburger buns or in large pita pockets.

# Tuna Steaks and Vegetable Kebabs

SERVES 2

*CAULIFLOWER AND ASPARAGUS ARE NOT USUALLY seen on skewers, but when liberally brushed with melted butter they become wonderful on the grill. Choose the most translucent tuna steaks you can find and be sure to give them a good sear on the grill for a flavorful crust. Served with rice, this recipe becomes a complete meal.*

Bring the grill to a high heat. Brush the tuna steaks with the olive oil and place on the grill. Sprinkle the top side of each steak with half of the dill. When the steaks are flipped, sprinkle the back sides with the other half.

Soak the skewers for 15 minutes. Thread all of the vegetables on skewers and place on the grill. Brush with the melted garlic butter.

Grill the tuna for 3 to 5 minutes and the vegetable kebabs for 8 to 10 minutes, or until done to your taste.

Serve the kebabs alongside the tuna steaks.

2   7- to 8-ounce ¾-inch to 1-inch thick tuna steaks
    Olive oil
1   teaspoon chopped fresh dill
4   10-inch wooden skewers
8   1-inch-diameter mushroom caps
1   red bell pepper, seeded, cut into 1-inch squares
1   green bell pepper, seeded, cut into 1-inch squares
1   yellow bell pepper, seeded, cut into 1-inch squares
1   zucchini, cut into ½-inch rounds
8   cherry tomatoes
4   to 6 cauliflower florets
6   asparagus tops (the top 2 inches)
½   cup unsalted butter, melted, with ½ teaspoon garlic powder added

# Portobellos with Olive Oil, Shallots and Garlic

SERVES 4

*PORTOBELLO MUSHROOMS, WHEN GRILLED, are as hearty and flavorful as any burger tossed on a barbecue. These are quick and simple and will accompany everything from fish to lamb without overpowering their flavors. Or, place these caps into a freshly baked roll, top with sautéed onions and a sprinkling of grated Parmesan cheese and you have the quintessential mushroom-burger!*

3 to 4 portobello mushroom caps, cleaned
Olive oil
2 to 3 large shallots, diced
4 to 5 large garlic cloves, minced
Salt and freshly ground pepper to taste

Brush both sides of each mushroom cap liberally with the olive oil. Sprinkle each with equal amounts of the shallots and garlic. Add the salt and pepper to taste.

Place the mushroom caps, top down, over a medium fire on a preheated grill for about 10 minutes (lower the grill lid, if you have one). The mushrooms are done when they soften up a bit (but don't let them get too soft). Serve hot.

# Grilled Corn and Pepper Relish

MAKES 2 CUPS

*WHEN SWEET SUMMER CORN is at its peak, double this recipe and make as much of this relish as possible. Place in decorative jars and give as gifts, or just seal and store in the refrigerator for your own use with any grilled meat or as an addition to stir-fried vegetables and rice. It can be frozen for about a month, extending the corn season that much longer.*

¼ cup olive oil

1 teaspoon garlic powder

½ teaspoon freshly ground pepper

3 ears corn, husks removed

1 red bell pepper, halved, seeded

3 green onions

1 tablespoon cider vinegar

2 teaspoons dark molasses

In a small bowl, combine the olive oil, garlic powder and freshly ground pepper. Place the corn, red pepper and green onions over a high heat on the grill. Brush the mixture all over the vegetables and turn them as they brown, about 3 to 5 minutes. Remove from the grill and set aside until cool enough to handle.

Using a large, sharp knife, cut the kernels off the cobs and place in a small mixing bowl. Dice the red pepper and slice the green onions and add to the bowl. Spoon the vinegar and molasses over the vegetables and toss to mix well. Cover with plastic wrap and chill for 1 hour before serving.

# Grilled Vegetables with Toasts

SERVES 6

*USING FRESH HERBS IS just one way of preparing this goat cheese spread. If you like your grilled food spicy, instead of oregano in the cheese, mix in a pinch of cayenne pepper and hot pepper sauce. Or, if you're looking for sweetness, swirl in a spoonful of chutney or homemade preserves.*

1   head garlic
    Aluminum foil
2   tablespoons olive oil
1   teaspoon coarse salt
2   tablespoons fresh lemon juice
2   tablespoons white wine vinegar
3   garlic cloves, minced
1   tablespoon dried oregano
1   teaspoon salt
1   teaspoon freshly ground pepper
1   cup olive oil
1   red bell pepper, halved, seeded
1   zucchini, halved lengthwise
1   yellow squash, halved lengthwise
6   ounces goat cheese
2   tablespoons chopped fresh oregano
12  ½-inch slices French bread, cut on bias

Trim the top off of the head of garlic. Place the garlic on the aluminum foil, pour 2 tablespoons of olive oil into its center and then sprinkle with the coarse salt. Wrap up in the foil. Place on the grill and lower the lid. Cook over medium-high heat for about 30 minutes and then remove from the grill and set aside.

In a small mixing bowl, whisk together the lemon juice, white wine vinegar, minced garlic, oregano, salt and pepper. While whisking constantly, slowly add the olive oil. Place the vegetables in a shallow baking dish and cover them with the vinaigrette. Turn to coat and then place cut side down, on the grill. Cook for 3 to 5 minutes and then turn. Cook for another 3 to 5 minutes and then return to the marinade.

Bring the goat cheese to room temperature and then in a small mixing bowl, using a rubber spatula, fold in the fresh oregano. Place the slices of bread on the grill and toast briefly, until sear marks appear. Turn and toast the other side.

When the garlic is cool enough to handle, squeeze out each individual clove from its paper onto a slice of toast. Spread with a knife and top with 1 to 2 tablespoons of the goat cheese mixture. Continue until all the goat cheese is used up.

Cut the pepper into long, ½-inch strips and the squash into ½-inch crescents. Mix and mound them in the center of a platter. Surround with the cheese-toasts and serve.

# Summer Squash and Pepper Slaw

*IF YOU'RE NOT A FAN OF CABBAGE, this is a milder, alternative slaw. You can shred in some yellow squash too if you'd like even more color. Fresh oregano or tarragon also go well with this if you want a flavor other than basil.*

1½ pounds zucchini

2 teaspoons salt

1 medium onion

1 red bell pepper, halved, seeded

¼ cup cider vinegar

½ cup olive oil

2 tablespoons mayonnaise

2 tablespoons chopped fresh basil

Cut the zucchini into 3-inch pieces. Using a hand grater, shred the zucchini lengthwise into long, thin strips. Place in a colander and sprinkle with the salt. Allow to drain for ½ hour.

While the zucchini is draining, cut the onion and red pepper into similar thin strips. Place in a mixing bowl and set aside.

Combine the vinegar, olive oil and mayonnaise and whisk until it is smooth. Add the basil. When the zucchini has drained, squeeze out any excess moisture and place in the bowl with the pepper and onion. Add the mayonnaise mixture and toss to coat.

# Ham and Cheese Portobello Mushrooms

SERVES 4

*IF YOU'RE AVOIDING BREADS, this recipe will cure any ham and cheese sandwich craving you may be having. Try a blend of cheeses—Cheddar, chevre and Swiss for a rich flavor, or feta, blue and Gouda for a true cheese hit. Either way, these flavors meld beautifully with the smokiness of the barbecue.*

| | |
|---|---|
| 4 | portobello mushroom caps |
| 3 | tablespoons Dijon-style mustard |
| 1 | teaspoon prepared horseradish |
| 1 | teaspoon honey |
| ½ | teaspoon freshly ground pepper |
| 1 | pound thinly sliced ham |
| 1 | pound thinly sliced Swiss cheese |

Place the mushrooms, cap side down, on the grill over high heat and close the lid. Cook for 3 to 5 minutes. Turn the caps over and move to the edge of the heat.

In a small mixing bowl, combine the mustard, horseradish, honey and pepper. Spoon the mixture evenly between the mushroom caps. Place the ham on the sauce and top with the cheese. Lower the lid of the grill and cook until the cheese is melted, about 5 minutes. Remove from the grill, cut each cap into quarters and serve.

Barbecues

# Corn on the Cob with Basil Butter

SERVES 6

*COOKING CORN ON THE GRILL keeps the whole meal preparation outside. The heat from cooking stays entirely out of the kitchen and you won't need to rush back and forth between a pot of boiling water on the stove for the corn and the grill for the meat. An added touch—a compound butter—will make your dinner guests feel as though this were an elegant meal made especially for them. It is very easy to prepare, can be shaped in a mold if you have one and can be made a day ahead. Try different fresh herbs like oregano or chives or a combination of them all.*

**BASIL BUTTER**

½ pound (2 sticks) unsalted butter

1 bunch fresh basil

½ teaspoon salt

**CORN**

6 ears corn

Salt and freshly ground pepper to taste

Aluminum foil

**FOR BUTTER:** Allow the butter to soften and place it in a mixing bowl. Rinse and dry the basil. Pick off the leaves and chop them fine. Add 2 or 3 tablespoons of chopped basil to the butter. Sprinkle with the salt and mix well.

Place the butter mixture into small ramekins, smooth the top and cover with plastic wrap. Chill until the butter is again firm.

**FOR CORN:** Peel back the green husks without removing them and remove the corn silk. Return half of the husk to each cob and salt and pepper. Cover the cobs with the remaining husks. Roll the corn on the cob in the foil and place on the grill over medium-high for 15 minutes, rolling from time to time to assure even cooking.

Keep the corn warm in the foil until it's time to serve. Serve with the basil butter.

# Curried Bananas

*YES, BANANAS! What a great addition to a mixed-grill plate. These spicy bananas go well with chicken or pork, or you can slice them up and mix with a salsa. If you want to try them plain, omit the seasonings and just brush them with the maple syrup or a little olive oil.*

4  firm bananas

1  tablespoon curry powder

1  teaspoon ground cumin

1  teaspoon ground ginger

½  teaspoon salt

½  teaspoon cayenne pepper

2  tablespoons maple syrup

Keeping the bananas in their skins, slice them in half, lengthwise. Bring the grill to a high heat. Combine the spices in a small mixing bowl. Rub on the flesh side of the bananas and place, flat side down, on the grill. Cook for about 2 minutes, until they begin to brown. Flip them over, brush with the maple syrup and cook for another 2 minutes. Remove from the grill and when they are cool enough to handle, remove the skins and serve.

# Wine Spiced Peaches

SERVES 4

*WHEN THE SEASON FOR TRULY tree-ripened peaches arrives, it is tempting to eat them with every meal. Here is an elegant, grown-up dessert that is terrific just as it is, or served with ice cream or over angel food cake. If you don't have a Sauternes available, use a Port or full-bodied red wine instead.*

1 pound slightly firm peaches, halved, pitted

1 cup Sauternes or similar sweet wine

¼ teaspoon ground cloves

¼ teaspoon ground cinnamon

¼ teaspoon ground ginger

¼ teaspoon ground mace

1 tablespoon sugar

¼ cup heavy cream

Place the peaches, cut side down over a medium-high fire on a preheated grill. Grill for 3 to 5 minutes, until sear marks appear on the flesh. Remove from the heat and set aside to cool down enough to handle.

In a small saucepot, bring the Sauternes, cloves, cinnamon, ginger, mace and sugar to a boil. Reduce by ⅓ and remove from the heat. Peel the skin off the peaches and place them in a wide, shallow bowl. Pour the wine mixture over the peaches, toss gently and let soak at room temperature for 2 hours, turning the peaches occasionally. Serve in individual bowls with a splash of cream. Can be refrigerated. Return to room temperature before serving.

# Index